THESE ARE THE GARMENTS

THE HIGH PRIEST'S GARMENTS.

THESE ARE
THE GARMENTS

*A Study of the Garments
of the High Priest of Israel*

by

CHARLES W. SLEMMING

CHRISTIAN LITERATURE CRUSADE
Fort Washington, Pennsylvania 19034

CHRISTIAN LITERATURE CRUSADE

U.S.A.
Box 1449, Fort Washington, PA 19034

CANADA
Box 189, Elgin, Ontario KOG 1EO

GREAT BRITAIN
51 The Dean, Alresford, Hants., SO24 9BJ

AUSTRALIA
P.O. Box 91, Pennant Hills, N.S.W. 2120

Revised August 1955
First American Edition 1974
This printing 1988
ISBN 0-87508-507-5

Printed in the United States of America

Dedicated to my wife
in acknowledgment of her great help
in preparing the manuscript

PREFACE

These lectures have been delivered verbally throughout Great Britain and the Continent of North America in Schools and Colleges as well as many Churches.

On every occasion there have been many testimonies of blessing received, of new light imparted, of difficult things made clear, of new appreciation of the Priestly Ministry of the Lord Jesus Christ.

Likewise has blessing come to an unknown company through the first edition of this book. As this second imprint goes forth on the ever widening circles of interest in a subject that has too long been neglected I trust that the Mediatorial work of the Lord Jesus Christ and His great Priestly Ministry on the behalf of His people may cause many to rejoice in the substance of the New Testament as it becomes manifest through the shadows of the Old Testament.

This New Edition has been completely revised and reset; and it is hoped that the illustrations specially drawn for the work, will increase the usefulness and interest of the book.

Yours because His,

CHARLES W. SLEMMING.

London and Chicago.

CONTENTS

THE GOLDEN CENSOR

CHAPTER I

THE AARONIC PRIESTHOOD

Exod. xxviii. and xxix.; *Heb.* iv. 14-16; v. 1-5; viii.

" Wherefore, holy brethren, partakers of the heavenly calling, consider the Apostle and High Priest of our profession, Christ Jesus." (Heb. iii. 1).

THE subject of the Priesthood, like many of the themes of Scripture, is inexhaustible. It scintillates as the twinkling stars of the heavens with glories which many have not yet beheld. Let us put our eye to the telescope of the Holy Spirit, and allow this subject to be brought nearer to our spiritual vision for, in so doing, we shall behold more of the grandeur and inexpressibleness of the " High Priest of our profession, Christ Jesus ".

Before meditating upon the subject of the Priestly Robes, we must know something concerning those who were consecrated to wear them — the priests of the Aaronic order.

For the sake of elucidation it would be well to differentiate between three terms which will make their re-occurrence throughout the book and which, to some, are only inter-changeable words. The terms are: " Priests ", " High Priests ", and " Great High Priest ".

(1) *Priests.* These were the members of the Aaronic family. The only claim for this office was sonship. There were many priests, the number varying according to the size of the family. Their work was to minister in holy things.

(2) *High Priests.* Aaron was the first. He was succeeded by his son, and so on, generation after generation. Only one high priest held office at a time; yet, according to Josephus, something more than eighty men officiated in this capacity between Aaron, the first, and Christ, the only reason for the change being death. This the Apostle tells us in Heb. vii. 23 : " And they truly were many priests, because they were not suffered to continue by reason of death." A changing priesthood meant an imperfect priesthood, so came the need of a

(3) *Great High Priest.* There was One and One only. He was the Lord Jesus Christ. He came not of the Aaronic order, not even of the tribe of Levi. He was a priest after the order of Melchisedec. He inherited His Priesthood from no one — He passed it on to none. He remains, He supersedes all others by reason of His endless life and, therefore, changeless ministry.

One further general reflection concerning the priesthood. It was progressive. Its development can be noticed throughout the Scriptures. In the beginning every individual man was his own priest and offered his own sacrifices, as did Adam, Cain, Abel, Noah, Abram, and others. In the Book of Exodus we find the head of the family officiating on the behalf of all who were in his house. " In the tenth day of this month, they shall take to them every man a lamb, according to the house of their fathers, a lamb for an house " (Exod. xii. 3). A further step of progression designated one tribe as separated from the twelve tribes for holy service, and from this one man was chosen to be priest. His name was Aaron.   He was assisted by his sons because of the magnitude of his ministry.   This Aaronic priesthood, for thus it was called, continued until the death of Christ in the days of Caiaphas, the High Priest.   Then it ended, for Christ passed within the veil and sat down at the right hand of the Majesty on high as the Great High Priest and took upon Himself the ministry of intercession for the whole Church of God.   The progress summarised is, therefore:

> A priest for himself.
> A priest for a family.
> A priest for a nation.
> A priest for the Church.

It is the priest for a nation we now consider.

The inauguration of this priesthood is recorded in Exod. xxviii. and xxix.   Remembering that these things " were written for our learning ", we will gather a few precious thoughts concerning our Great High Priest, and a few practical lessons for ourselves.

The first verse introduces a man who was

CALLED.   " And take thou unto thee Aaron, thy brother, and his sons with him, from among the children of Israel, that he may minister unto Me in the priest's Office." (Exod. xxviii. 1).

To receive a Divine call is a matter of first importance. Korah and his companions evidently believed this, but were unwise in the way they handled the matter, for in Num. xvi. and xvii. instead of ascertaining the actual facts, they laid grievous charges against Moses, accusing him of making the calling a family matter and an outcome of pride.   This resulted in a rebellion in which two hundred and fifty princes took sides with Korah, Dathan, and Abiram, bringing upon themselves a plague from the Lord. It was after this rebellion that God revealed through Aaron's rod, which He caused to bud, blossom, and yield fruit, that the appointment of Aaron was of God.[1]

Christ Himself had nothing of a selfish nature, neither did He choose for Himself His mission of life. The Apostle makes this very clear in Heb. v. 1-6, 10 : " For every high priest taken from among men is ordained for men in things pertaining to God, that he may offer both gifts and sacrifices for sins : Who can have compassion on the ignorant, and on them that are out of the way; for that he himself also is compassed with infirmity. And by reason hereof he ought, as for the people, so also for himself, to offer for sins. And no man taketh this honour unto himself, but he that is called of God, as was Aaron. So also Christ glorified not Himself to be made an high priest; but He that said unto Him, Thou art My Son, to-day have I begotten Thee. As He saith also in another place, Thou art a priest for ever after the order of Melchisedec . . . . Called of God an high priest after the order of Melchisedec."

If such a calling became necessary for the priesthood of the old order and if Christ was called of God, how much more should not those who are engaged in the work of the ministry assure themselves that they are there because of a Divine call. Many men are in the ministry to-day, not because of election by a synod, nor because of ordination by the laying on of hands by the presbytery (they did it acting for God as did Moses), but because they were conscious that the Lord had already called and ordained them. The human sphere must always stand second to

[1] See Author's book : **Made According to Pattern**, chap. xviii

God. Alas, so many look upon the work of the ministry as a profession with the result they are doing nothing which is really vital, and surely the vital part of God's work is seeing men won for Christ through a real evangelism, and also establishing men in their " most holy faith " through the unfolding of the Word of God, and the encouraging of God's people to a deeper life of sanctification.

There is a still broader sense in which to observe this call, by leaving the high priest for a moment and remembering that we are all of us called to be priests unto God. Paul says : " I, therefore, the prisoner of the Lord, beseech you that ye walk worthy of the vocation wherewith ye are called, with all lowliness and meekness, with longsuffering, forbearing one another in love ". (Ephes. iv. 1-2). And again : " . . . God hath from the beginning chosen you to salvation through sanctification of the Spirit and belief of the truth : Whereunto He called you by our gospel, to the obtaining of the glory of our Lord Jesus Christ. Therefore, brethren, stand fast, and hold the traditions which ye have been taught, whether by word, or our epistle " (2 Thes. ii. 13-15). We are all, therefore, called to " walk worthy " and to " stand fast ". The call was followed by

CLEANSING. " And Aaron and his sons thou shalt bring unto the door of the tabernacle of the congregation, and shalt wash them with water " (Exod. xxix. 4). This relates to the priesthood. Therefore this washing does not refer to salvation. An unsaved man would never be called to the ministry. It is good always to remember that the washing which brings cleansing from sin is in the Blood, not in water, water being a type of the Word of God : " Now ye are clean through the Word which I have spoken unto you " (John xv. 3), and " Wherewithal shall

B

a young man cleanse his way? By taking heed thereto according to Thy Word " (Ps. cxix. 9) etc. Anyone called to God's service should become immersed into the Word of God for his own sanctification as well as for his spiritual equipment to instruct others. Christ Himself, Who became the Great High Priest, was the Word Incarnate.

We are not told how the washing was done, except that it was public, in the presence of the whole congregation, and we presume it was at the brazen laver. Ministers of God who would take a public stand for God's Word, and Theological Colleges, too, that would use the Bible as their only text book, would find God's Word would wash away any doubts and criticisms, divesting us of all self-opinion and leaving as standing as good fundamentalists. The next two verses tell us how they were

CLOTHED. " And thou shalt take the garments, and put upon Aaron the coat, and the robe of the ephod, and the ephod, and the breastplate, and gird him with the curious girdle of the ephod : And thou shalt put the mitre upon his head, and put the holy crown upon the mitre " (Exod. xxix. 5-6).

The detail of these garments is the theme of this book, so we shall not speak of them just at this point. But if on may be permitted to stray from the strict textual interpretation for a moment in order to glance at these things symbolically, it will possibly be not without profit. These garments were actually part of Aaron's consecration, as is stated in Exod. xxviii. 3. " . . . . that they may make Aaron's garments to consecrate him, that he may minister unto Me in the priest's office."

Bearing in mind these three truths of " Calling ", " Cleansing ", and " Clothng " we will look again at Him Who is our Great High Priest at the time when He commenced His early ministry. John the Baptist announced Him as the One Who was called of God, saying: " Behold, the Lamb of God " (John i. 29). " Then cometh Jesus from Galilee to Jordan unto John, to be baptised of him " (Matt. iii. 13). Although baptism is a symbolic act of death yet for the moment we can see a beautiful picture of the public washing of Him Who was about to take up His public ministry. " And Jesus, when He was baptised, went up *straightway* out of the water; and, lo, the heavens were opened unto Him, and He saw the Spirit of God descending like a dove, and lighting upon Him " (Matt. iii. 16). John, writing of this incident himself, said: " And I knew Him not: but He that sent me to baptise with water, the same said unto me, Upon Whom thou shalt see the Spirit descending and remaining on Him, the same is He which baptiseth with the Holy Ghost " (John i. 33). Surely this is the immediate clothing that makes for consecration. It is the clothing upon with the mantle of the Holy Ghost, the final equipment for powerful service. Thus was the order for Old Testament service — and thus the order for New Testament ministry. Have things changed to-day? With deep conviction we say " No!"

CONSECRATION. " . . . . And thou shalt consecrate Aaron and his sons " (Exod. xxix. 9). The whole detail of the ordinance of this consecration is found in *vv.* 10 to 36. The outstanding peculiarity of this ceremony is that which relates to the application of the blood. " Then shalt thou kill the ram, and take of his blood, and put it upon the tip of the right ear of Aaron, and upon the tip of the right ear of his sons, and upon the thumb of their right hand, and upon the great toe of their right foot, and sprinkle the blood upon the altar round about."

There comes to one's mind how Peter smote off the ear of Malchus, the High Priest's servant, in a spirit of revenge. Why that part of the anatomy we do not know. Also of how Adoni-Bezek cut off the thumbs and great toes of seventy kings he had subdued, and then how he himself suffered the same fate (Judges i. 6-7). The reason for committing such a cruel act appears to be one of moral disposition. It has been stated: " Thumbs were cut off to incapacitate the hand from using the bow; great toes to render the gait uncertain." In the act of consecration by anointing these particular members with blood we have a picture which is the reverse. Instead of being incapacitated by amputation, these priests were to have each member quickened by consecration. The ear was anointed so that it might be sensitive to the law of God, and that it might hear the confessions of the people's sins for God and not for gossip. The thumb was anointed that it might do the bidding of God, and that it might handle the offerings of the people for God and not for gold. The great toe was anointed that it might walk in the ways of God, and that it might minister in service for God and not for gain.

The Apostle writing to the Hebrews tells them that the priests must be

COMPASSIONATE. " Who can have compassion on the ignorant, and on them that are out of the way " (Heb. v. 2). This statement lends itself to much meditation. Such a characteristic was truly Christ's, as stated in the previous chapter. " For we have not an High Priest which cannot be touched with the feeling of our infirmities; but was in all points tempted like as we are, yet without sin " (Heb. iv. 15). How often do we read in the gospel story: " And He was moved with compassion." We, too, shall do little for men unless we have a sympathetic and compassionate heart and know how to bear each other's burdens, to weep with those who weep, and to rejoice with those that rejoice.

Finally, the priests were

COMMISSIONED. Their commission is to be found throughout the Book of Leviticus. They had to obey all the instructions of the Lord God and to become, through the sacrifices, intercessors between God and man. Christ to-day is fulfilling His Priestly functions on our behalf, and as His children we must fulfil ours.

CHAPTER II

Gen. xiv.; *Ps*. cx.; *Heb*. vii.

" For this Melchisedec, King of Salem, priest of the most High
God, who met Abraham returning from the slaughter of the kings,
and blessed him; To whom also Abraham gave a tenth part of all,
first being by interpretation King of righteousness, and after that
also King of Salem, which is, King of peace; without father, without mother, without descent, having neither beginning of days,
nor end of life; but made like unto the Son of God, abideth a
priest continually. Now consider how great this man was, unto
whom even the patriarch Abraham gave a tenth of the spoils. And
verily they that are of the sons of Levi, who receive the office of
the priesthood, have a commandment to take tithes of the people
according to the law, that is, of their brethren, though they come
out of the loins of Abraham : But he whose descent is not counted
from them received tithes of Abraham, and blessed him that had
the promises. And without all contradiction the less is blessed of
the better " (Heb. vii. 1-7).

WHILE the Aaronic priesthood was God-ordained and
sufficient for the time then being, it was by no means perfect because it was functioned by men who knew sin and,
therefore, were subjected to death. This meant a priesthood that was ever changing, with all that was resultant.
But God knew this, and had planned a more perfect
priesthood which could only come into being in the fulness of His time, for God works to schedule. This is seen
from many Scriptures, e.g.: " But when the *fulness* of
the time was come, God sent forth His Son, made of a
woman, made under the law " (Gal. iv. 4). " Jesus saith
unto her, Woman, what have I to do with thee? Mine
hour is not yet come " (John ii. 4). " But no man laid
hands on Him, because His *hour* was not yet come "
(John vii. 30). Jesus praying in John xvii. 1 says:
" Father, the *hour* is come." To His disciples He said :

" It is not for you to know the *times* or the *seasons,* which the Father hath put in His own power " (Acts i. 7). In the next chapter are the words : " And when the *day* of Pentecost was fully come " (Acts ii. 1). This applies also in His Second Advent : " But of that *day* and *hour* knoweth no man, no, not the angels of heaven, but my Father only " (Matt. xxiv. 36). One other reference tells us that : " He hath appointed a *day,* in the which He will judge the world in righteousness " (Acts xvii. 31). Although that perfect Priest was Jesus, and although His Priestly ministry was not to commence until after His death when He ascended on high, yet God gave a very vivid picture of the nature of this priesthood nearly two thousand years before it was established, and just over four hundred years before the Aaronic order was instituted. Maybe the meaning that lay behind the sudden appearing and disappearing of Melchisedec was not realised then, not until it was uttered by David in one of his Messianic prophecies : " Thou art a priest for ever after the order of Melchizedek " (Ps. cx. 4). The Apostle makes much more of it in Hebrews.

The book of Hebrews is considered one of the grandest and ablest arguments or demonstrations of reasoning ability in the whole of literature. The Apostle, whom we believe was Paul, being faced with Judaism which was a yoke of bondage to the Christian faith, as he states in Galatians, and realising how difficult it was for those Hebrew Christians to abandon all their traditions and, at the same time, possibly knowing that the predicted day was not far distant when the Temple would be destroyed and they scattered the world over, thus ending suddenly much to which they were holding, most masterfully seeks to wean them from the " old " and woo them to the " new " by asking them to consider the Apostle and High

Priest of their profession, Christ Jesus. He reminds them of the faithfulness of Moses and expounds to them the greater worthiness of Christ. From Moses he passes on to Aaron and the priesthood, showing how they failed to satisfy the requirements of men. Then, coming to the middle of the book, he takes up the subject of Melchisedec and shows him to be a more perfect priest than any of the Aaronic family, finally declaring that Christ was not only after the order of Melchisedec but· that He superseded all, for He opened a " new and living way " by His Death so that we could " draw nigh with a true heart, in full assurance of faith ".

Let us now consider what the difference is between the Aaronic priesthood and the Melchisedec priesthood. The question is naturally asked : " Who was Melchisedec?" Many have suggested that he was some super-human person, some believing him to be Christ. The text of Scripture is quite opposed to such suggestions and, if read correctly, everything is quite logical. Some think that it is not logical for a man to have no parents, and to have no birth nor death — and rightly so! But how does the Bible state it? It is most important always to know where we are reading and about what we are reading, because things are often relative to something else. To understand a text we *must* know the context, otherwise our interpretation may be a pretext. We must ask ourselves such questions as : " Who is speaking? God or man. Is it the Old Testament or the New Testament? It is an historical statement or is it of doctrinal intent?" By doing this we shall be more able to " rightly divide the Word of Truth ".

With these things in mind then, two statements are to be considered. They are Gen. xiv. 18-20 and Heb. vii. 1-3. Both are stated by man. One is written in the Old

Testament, the other in the New Testament. The first is a definite historical record, the second is an exegesis of the first. Written in the two Testaments, the statements are about two thousand years apart — the one is historical, the other is not. The historical account, which is a statement of facts, reads thus: " And Melchizedek king of Salem brought forth bread and wine: and he was the priest of the Most High God. And he blessed him, and said, Blessed be Abram of the Most High God, possessor of heaven and earth: And Blessed be the Most High God, which hath delivered thine enemies into thy hand. And he gave him tithes of all " (Gen. xiv. 18-20). There is nothing strange nor super-human in that statement. Nothing whatever! Reading the whole chapter, it concerns a battle, a defeat, a victory and a blessing. It gives the names of ten kings and the districts or cities over which they reigned. Amongst these names is Melchizedek, king of Salem. Salem will be found on any map of that period as the ancient name for Jerusalem which was at that time Canaanitish. It is all so very matter-of-fact. We know then who Melchizedek was — a godly king of the very ancient city of Jerusalem, who also officiated as a priest unto God, and whom God sent out to refresh and bless Abram.

The second statement is " For this Melchisedec, king of Salem, priest of the Most High God, who met Abraham returning from the slaughter of the kings, and blessed him: To whom also Abraham gave a tenth part of all; first being by interpretation King of righteousness, and after that also King of Salem, which is, King of peace; Without father, without mother, without descent, having neither beginning of days, nor end of life; but made like unto the Son of God; abideth a priest continually " (Heb. vii. 1-3). The first verse and the first clause of the second verse are a reiteration of the Old Testament statements; the remainder is doctrine being established on it, therefore not necessarily a statement of historical fact.   In this exegesis comes the expression which has baffled many.   " Without father, without mother, etc." but it is an allusion. To paraphrase it, the Apostle says: " Here is a king and a priest, therefore a person of notability, yet, contrary to all Eastern custom, you cannot tell who his parents were nor when he was born, nor yet have you any record of his death. Then, turning to the subject of the Aaronic priesthood, he reasons that the law demanded not character but sonship. A man must inherit his priestly rights from his father and in turn he must pass them on to his son; so it was ever changing so far as character, conduct, ability, etc., of the man were concerned. But from whom did Melchisedec inherit his priesthood?   So far as they knew from no one. To whom did he pass it on? They had no record, and so he stood doctrinally: " A priest for ever," a type of a kingly and changeless priesthood.   This is the " order " to which Christ belongs. The whole chapter reasons it out to the very last.

Now consider the characteristics of this new " order ".

It was unique. There were many High Priests and Priests who officiated under the Aaronic Presthood, all of them subjected to death, but only one, Melchisedec, stood out like the moon against the stars of the night. But when the morning of the New Testament came, the One Great High Priest — Jesus — arose like the sun, so subduing all other lights.   Others had only borne a dim reflection of Him.

It was universal. While the Aaronic Priesthood was established for a nation, Israel — and for a period, until Christ should come — Melchisedec came before Jews and

Gentiles existed as separate people, and very early in time. When the greater than Melchisedec came, He made Jew and Gentile one again in Himself. For in Christ Jesus there is neither Jew nor Gentile, all are one in Him. His priestly work is world-wide and is age long, as He intercedes for all believers everywhere, irrespective of nation or denomination. He is the one Mediator between God and men.

It was unchanging. That Melchisedec in all his greatness was only a type is pointed out by the Apostle as he shows the need of a change from the changeable to the changeless in the words: " If therefore perfection were by the Levitical priesthood (for under it the people received the law), what further need was there that another priest should rise after the order of Melchisedec, and not be called after the order of Aaron? For the priesthood being changed, there is made of necessity a change also of the law. For He of whom these things are spoken pertaineth to another tribe, of which no man gave attendance at the altar. For it is evident that our Lord sprang out of Juda; of which tribe Moses spake nothing concerning priesthood. And it is yet far more evident; for that after the similitude of Melchisedec there ariseth another priest, Who is made, not after the law of a carnal commandment, but after the power of an endless life. For He testifieth, Thou art a priest for ever after the order of Melchisedec " (Heb. vii. 11-17). Then again in *v.* 24: " But this man, because He continueth ever, hath an unchangeable priesthood."

As one High Priest succeeded the other, the carnal commandment said he must be a son of the former but no law could alter or control the character of that son. One priest might be willing, but not the next; one might be kind and loving, another irritable; one devoted the other half-hearted; one man might be understanding, but his successor have little feeling. But we have an unchanging priest — " Jesus Christ, the same yesterday, and to-day, and for ever." He is kind, gentle, and One Who is touched with the feelings of our infirmities. He is consecrated by an oath which cannot be altered. This indeed should make our souls cry out: " Hallelujah, what a Saviour!"

One thing remains with which to conclude this chapter.

It was uniform. Both Melchisedec and Christ bear the same names and office. They are (1) *King*. Melchisedec had royal blood in his veins, he claimed the title of kingship. Aaron could make no such claim, neither could any one else of the tribe of Levi, it was a holy tribe. Kingship was confined mostly to Judah, from which tribe came David, Solomon, and others. It was Uzzah, king of Judah, who attempted to offer incense at the Golden Altar and was smitten with leprosy. Only one king out of Judah ever became a priest and that was Christ, the Lion of the tribe of Judah, hence He was not of the Aaronic order, but above it. He was the Royal Priest. (2) *Righteousness.* " King of Righteousness " was the meaning of the name Melchisedec. Christ was more than King of Israel. He, too, was King of Righteousness. His Name was Jehovah Tsidkenu, " The Lord our Righteousness ". He preached righteousness, He lived righteously. He reigns in righteousness, and all His people He makes righteous. (3) *Peace.* As King of Salem, or King of Peace, Melchisedec met Abram on his return from warfare, having gained a great victory. One has no need to enlarge on this wonderful attribute of Christ, the King of Peace, He Who has destroyed our enemies and Who reigns in peace in the hearts of His children.

(4) *Priest of the Most High God.* This is stated of both, and describes their great office.

CHAPTER III

INTRODUCTION TO THE GARMENTS

Exod. xxviii. 1-43; *Lev.* viii. 6-9

" And take thou unto thee Aaron thy brother, and his sons with him, from among the children of Israel, that he may minister unto Me in the priest's office, even Aaron, Nadab and Abihu, Eleazar and Ithamar, Aaron's sons. And thou shalt make holy garments for Aaron thy brother for glory and beauty. And thou shalt speak unto all that are wise hearted, whom I have filled with the spirit of wisdom, that they may make Aaron's garments to consecrate him, that he may minister unto Me in the priest's office. And these are the garments which they shall make; a breastplate and an ephod, and a robe, and a broidered coat, a mitre, and a girdle : and they shall make holy garments for Aaron thy brother, and his sons, that he may minister unto Me in the priest's office. And they shall take gold, and blue, and purple, and scarlet, and fine linen " (Exod. xxviii. 1-5).

MUCH detail is subscribed to the making of the garments for Aaron and his sons, so much so that one's attention is naturally drawn to the meaning of it all. As Scripture tells us that " all things are written for our learning ", it is necessarily our duty to find out that which the Lord desires us to know. As the High Prest was a type of the Great High Priest, Jesus, so the garments of the High Priest were typical of the character of Jesus Christ. Likewise, as the sons of the High Priests were priests and as we who are the sons of God are called to be priests, even so the dress of the priests typifies the character of the believers. The chief lesson to be learned from these robes is, therefore, the character which is essentially Christ's, and then the character of believers in their relationship to Him.

In Exodus chapters xxv to xxx the details of the tabernacle are fully prescribed. Two of the intermediate

chapters are occupied with the instructions concerning
the priestly clothing and consecration. So the priesthood,
with its robes and ritual, was not an afterthought but the
very life of the tabernacle service. The tabernacle without the priesthood would be barren and void. The
ministry, therefore, must not be disdained, because it has
been God ordained; while the minister himself must be
enveloped in all that for which God and the Church
stand. The ministry must be recognised by those who
enter it as an high calling demanding the very best that
man possesses, and then it must be recognised by the
people as a God-chosen avenue for conveying His Truth
to the Church through an honest handling of the Word
of God.

The quality of the whole of these vestments, whether
it was texture or material or workmanship, was the very
best of its kind — *fine* linen, *pure* gold, *precious* stones,
costly ointment, *cunning* workmanship, all used by *wise*
hearts. This was because it was all a type of Christ's
character, and nothing but the very highest quality will
do to portray Him Who was an example of humanity
as it ought to be and as one day it will be. Jesus was
Divinity manifested in humanity so that humanity might
take on Divinity by becoming the sons of God. Nothing
but that which was unalloyed could represent Him Who
was " holy, harmless, undefiled, separate from sinners ";
Who was " Wisdom, righteousness, sanctification, and
redemption ". Again He was the personification of
" love, joy, peace, long-suffering, gentleness, goodness,
faith, meekness, and temperance ". Majesty and humble-
ness were blended in Him. Mercy and truth met in Him
and kissed each other. Humanity and Divinity har-
monised only in the High Priest of our profession.

Aaron was clothed upon with these garments, thus

fitting him for the office to which he was called, and covering him with a dignity he did not otherwise possess, for the robes were part of his consecration. What a contrast to the Lord Jesus Christ. Character, not clothes, fitted Him; His glory and dignity He had from eternity, they were essentially His.

It is inspiring to meditate upon the thought given us in the first verse of Exodus xxviii: " And take thou unto thee *Aaron thy brother, and his sons* with him, from among the children of Israel, that *he* may minister unto Me in the priest's office, even Aaron, Nadab and Abihu, Eleazar and Ithamar, Aaron's sons." God chose five men, Aaron and his four sons, and then referred to them in the singular pronoun " that *he* may minister ". The ministries of these five men were inseparably wrapped up in each other, so that God saw them as one. Aaron did not minister without the priests (except on the Day of Atonement), and the priests could not minister without their high priest. This is all very wonderful, for Christ does not minister alone. He has called us to be priests that we might share in the ministry of intercession. We, too, like the priests of old, cannot minister apart from our Great High Priest upon Whom we have to depend at all times. These five men thus working together remind us that even behind the law, God was seeking to show forth His grace. (Five is the typical number of grace).

The vestments included a coat with its girdle, a robe, an ephod, the curious girdle, the breastplate with Urim and Thummim, the Mitre and the Holy Crown, and afterwards there is mention of breeches. This is not the order laid down in Exodus, there is no repeated order there. It is in this order that we shall now deal with the subject, because this would be the order in which the priest would put them on, and is found in Lev. viii. 7-9. We begin, therefore, with the undergarment, or the foundation, and work outwards.

One final word of introduction.   The priest in his robes of " glory and beauty " was adorned in harmony with his surroundings — the tabernacle; the same colours, some of the same materials, the same skilful workmanship.   This again reminds us of the great fact that God loves harmony, and that all His work is harmonious. Could we imagine it otherwise?   Yet alas !   We see much today in Christian work that is discord.   Somehow, a dance and worship do not blend, there is no harmony in Church music and jazz.   A concert and the singing of Psalms jar, a whist-drive and any of the Divine ordinances of the Church are a great contrast.   Yet all these things are indulged in by some, and are held under the same name of " Church ".   Let us come to a holy God as holy people, let the reverence of the sanctuary pervade everything.   " Let the words of my mouth, and the meditation of my heart, be acceptable in Thy sight, O Lord, my strength, and my redeemer " (Ps. xix. 14).

THE SHOULDER STONES. (*See page* 62).

CHAPTER IV

THE LINEN COAT

Exod. xxviii. 39; xxxix. 27

" And thou shalt embroider the coat of fine linen, and thou shalt make the mitre of fine linen, and thou shalt make the girdle of needlework." (Exod. xviii. 39).

" And they made coats of fine linen of woven work for Aaron, and for his sons " (Exod. xxxix. 27).

" And Moses brought Aaron and his sons, and washed them with water. And he put upon him the coat, and girded him with the girdle . . . " (Lev. viii. 6-7.)

THE COAT " And thou shalt embroider the coat." There was nothing plain or ordinary in the things which God planned; nature tells us so, the harmony of the Bible declares it, and so does everything else. Gazing at this coat from the distance, and especially in contrast with the other garments, it would appear quite ordinary, but upon a closer examination there was skill and beauty attached to the make up of the fabric. The root word used for " embroider " gives us the same idea as our modern " damask ", an embroidery not worked on but skilfully worked into the material. To the many who take a casual glance at the " Jesus of Nazareth " and the " Man of Galilee " they see an ordinary yet good man; but study that character, look into that life, note those good works, and meditate upon His words. Here is no ordinary person, even though He is found in fashion as a man. There is a Divine pattern most intrinsically worked into the human frame which reveals Him to be the Son of God.

Three more words make the total sum of what we are told about this coat—" of fine linen ". Only nine words in all, but what a mine of wealth! It is like the comparatively small telescope which, when put to the eye, will bring to your vision a great panorama of beauty.

This " fine linen ", such as cannot be purchased or even manufactured today, was an Egyptian art which died with the Egyptians. Sir J. Gardner Wilkinson, D.C.L., F.R.S., etc., in his book *Manners and Customs of the Ancient Egyptians,* tells us quite a lot about this wonderful fabric: " The Egyptians were always celebrated for their manufacture of linen and other cloths, and the produce of their looms was exported to, and eagerly purchased by, foreign nations. The fine linen and embroidered work, the yarn and woollen stuffs of the upper and lower country are frequently mentioned, and were highly esteemed " (Vol. II. p. 72). " Nor was the praise bestowed upon that manufacture unmerited; and the quality of one piece of linen found near Memphis fully justifies it, and excites equal admiration at the present day, being to the touch comparable to silk, and not inferior in texture to our finest cambric " (Vol. II. p. 75). But what has Egypt and its art to do with the priestly garments? It is just another proof of the accuracy of the Bible, for how came these Israelites in a wilderness to possess such material? They spoiled the Egyptians! This we are told in Exod. iii. 22.

Not only did this material have such a *fine* texture, which holds the same typology as the *fine* flour of the shewbread and the *fine* flour of the Meal (Meat) Offering, but we have every reason to believe that it was pure white. What a matchless picture of Him Who in Rev. i. 13-14 was " clothed with a garment down to the foot " and Whose " hairs were white like wool, as white as snow "; enveloped in a spotless purity and the essence of perfect righteousness. Thus we see our Great High Priest, and thus He was when He was found in fashion as a man. See what Scriptures say of Him; hear what those who witnessed His life and death record. All who spoke truthfully attested to His perfect and flawless life. Meeting temptation in the wilderness He overcame it and remained sinless (Luke iv); associating with sinners He was not contaminated (Matt. ix. 10-13); mixing amongst publicans and harlots, He stood pure and holy (Matt. xxi. 31-32; John viii. 2-11). As in His life, so in His death. For here are the verdicts of the leading characters in that greatest drama of all time:

Pilate: " I find *no fault* in this man " (Luke xxiii. 4).

Pilate's wife: " Have thou nothing to do with that *just* Man " (Matt. xxvii. 19).

Judas: " I have sinned in that I have betrayed the *innocent* blood " (Matt. xxvii. 4).

The Malefactor: " This Man hath done *nothing amiss*" (Luke xxiii. 41).

The Centurion: " Certainly this was a *righteous* Man " (Luke xxiii. 47).

God: " My *beloved* Son, in Whom I am well pleased " (Matt. xvii. 5).

The apostles writing in after years declared with no uncertainty the same thing:

Peter: " But ye denied the *Holy One* and the *Just*, and desired a murderer to be granted unto you " (Acts iii. 14).

Stephen: " Which of the prophets have not your fathers persecuted? And they have slain them which shewed before of the coming of the *Just One;* of whom ye have been now the betrayers and murderers " (Acts vii. 52).

Ananias: " And he said, the God of our fathers hath chosen thee, that thou shouldest know His will, and see that *Just One,* and shouldest hear the voice of His mouth" (Acts xxii. 14). (From Paul).

Paul? : " . . . but was in all points tempted like as we are, yet *without sin* " (Heb. iv. 15).

Leaving the thought of righteousness and holiness for a moment, profit will be gained by considering the Hebrew word here translated " coat ". It is " Kethoneth ". The root meaning of this word is twofold—" To cover " or " to hide ". It is exactly the same word as is used in Gen. iii. 21, and there translated " coats ". In the literal translation the verse reads : " And Jehovah God doth make to the man, and to his wife coats (Kethoneths) of skin and doth clothe them." (Note that in the original the word is " skin ". It is singular and not plural as in our Authorised Version. This suggests that one sacrifice was sufficient for both). When Adam sinned he tried first *to cover* his nakedness with leaves, and then he sought *to hide* behind the trees of the garden. Both were of no avail before the penetrating eye of a righteous God Who was demanding a strict adherence to His word. Then it was He made for them a Kethoneth *to cover* their sin and *to hide* their shame. This we know was only accomplished through the death of another, and also through the shedding of blood.

Thus in this first garment of the High Priest is secreted some of the wonder of the holiness and righteousness of the Christ.

In this one garment High Priest and Priests were alike, for all wore the white coat with this one difference. It was the High Priest's undergarment, but with the priest it was his only garment. (With this white coat was included all that was fine linen, viz.: girdle, bonnet, and breeches). Righteousness was the foundation of all else that Christ was, but the only merit claimed by a believer is an imputed righteousness. As the sons of God such have been clothed in His righteousness because they have been washed in His Blood. Having received this imputed righteousness we are able to say with the prophet Isaiah: " I will greatly rejoice in the Lord, my soul shall be joyful in my God: for He hath clothed me with the garments of salvation, He hath covered me with the robe of righteousness . . . " (Isa. lxi. 10); whilst we listen to the Lord God saying: " Ye shall therefore be holy, for I am holy " (Lev. xi. 45). Peter repeats this injunction in the New Testament (1 Peter i. 16).

Notice that the coat was put on the moment the priest was washed, but not so with Jesus. It was never put upon Him. When He had divested Himself of everything that He had with the Father and in eternity, when He had stripped Himself of His glory and had made Himself of no reputation, this character remained inseparably His. He *was* holy, He *was* righteous, and none could rob Him. Oh, the glory and the wonder of it all!

Attached to this embroidered coat was

The Girdle. This is nearly always a symbol of service, the girded loins denoting readiness for action. This must always be the attitude of the priest and it is certainly true of Christ, for of Him it is said: " He *ever* maketh intercession for us." This linen girdle was not the curious girdle of *v.* 8. It was attached to the undergarment and so was not seen except on the Day of Atonement. Nonetheless it was there girding the loins. Perhaps we are not always conscious that the Lord is ministering on our behalf especially when we see no outward evidence, but we can encourage our hearts with the fact that He is always working on our behalf. Isaiah speaking of Christ says: " But with righteousness shall He judge the poor, and reprove with equity for the meek of the earth : and He shall smite the earth with the rod of His mouth, and with the breath of His lips shall He slay the wicked. And righteousness shall be the girdle of His loins, and faithfulness the girdle of His reins " (Isa. xi. 4-5). Paul referring to the believers calls them to put on the " girdle of truth " (Eph. vi). Therefore, Christ and His people are not only clothed with righteousness but that righteousness is bound to us by the righteous, eternal and unalterable Word of the Living God. This coat with its girdle, as well as the more gorgeous apparel, is called a robe of glory and beauty.

THE BELLS AND THE POMEGRANATES AROUND THE HEM OF THE HIGH PRIEST'S ROBE.

CHAPTER V

THE ROBE OF THE EPHOD

Exod. xxviii. 31-35; xxxix. 22-26

" And thou shalt make the robe of the ephod all of blue. And there shall be an hole in the top of it, in the midst thereof: it shall have a binding of woven work round about the hole of it, as it were the hole of an habergeon, that it be not rent. And beneath upon the hem of it thou shalt make pomegranates of blue, and of purple, and of scarlet, round about the hem thereof: and bells of gold between them round about: A golden bell and a pomegranate, a golden bell and a pomegranate, upon the hem of the robe round about: and it shall be upon Aaron to minister: and his sound shall be heard when he goeth in unto the holy place before the Lord, and when he cometh out, that he die not " (Exod. xxviii. 31-35).

THE ROBE of the ephod is the first of the vestments which belongs expressly to the High Priest.

This is the first time that the word " robe " occurs in Scripture, and it stands in contrast to the coat. It is to be noted that certain words and expressions which we use in a very general way are used in Scripture in a definitely specific way. The coat is a garment used expressly for the purpose of covering. The robe is always worn as the symbol of office and authority. This is readily seen to be true in the following Scriptures: " And the men of

36

David said unto him, Behold the day of which the Lord said unto thee, Behold, I will deliver thine enemy into thine hand, that thou mayest do to him as it shall seem good unto thee. Then David arose, and cut off the skirt of Saul's robe privily " (1 Sam. xxiv. 4). " I put on righteousness, and it clothed me: my judgment was as a robe and a diadem " (Job xxix. 14). " Then all the princes of the sea shall come down from their thrones, and lay away their robes, and put off their embroidered garments: they shall clothe themselves with trembling; they shall sit upon the ground, and shall tremble at every moment, and be astonished at thee " (Ezek. xxvi. 16).

In these references, as in all others, the robe carries with it dignity, and is also that which belongs to royalty. You cannot imagine a person in robes being other than dignified. Have you seen a judge wearing all his judicial robes running for a bus? Can you imagine a Lord Mayor wearing all his regalia romping on the sands with his children? No! The robes dignify a man for the office he holds. Even so Aaron was robed for office and his position commanded respect. Every servant of the Lord who ministers in holy things should himself respect his office and should be respected because of his office.

With regard to the robe belonging to a royal personage, one New Testament Scripture will suffice. " And they stripped Him, and put on Him a scarlet *robe* . . . and mocked Him, saying, Hail *King* of the Jews " (Matt. xxvii. 28-29). Aaron had no claim to kingship. His robes only dignified him in his priestly capacity. Jesus dignified the realm of royalty as well as that of priesthood.

ROYALTY is the underlying truth of the garment so far as its name is concerned, and reveals that royalty which belonged to the Christ of God, the Great High

Priest. This priestly office of Christ superseded that of Aaron, being of the Melchisedec order — of an endless life.

Here then is a very wonderful blending of truth brought out in garments. Melchisedec was *king* of *righteousness* and *king* of *peace*. The robe of the ephod having upon it as an ornamentation the symbols of peace (as will presently be seen) is placed upon a man already wearing the white coat, the emblem of righteousness. Thus the man foreshadowed Him Who never wore the emblem of, but in reality was, the King of Righteousness and the King of Peace.

It is perhaps of some importance to take notice of one of those striking omissions of Scripture. Often amidst minute and detailed description of a thing or a scene, some more important matter appears to be omitted. In this case nothing is said as to the nature of the material used. It is not revealed whether the garment was of linen, silk, wool, goat's hair, camel's hair, or any other fabric worn by Eastern people. The Scripture statement is: "And thou shalt make the robe of the ephod all (of) blue" (*v.* 31). The emphasis seems to be on the colour rather than the texture. This is a peculiarity of Scripture in its original text. Henry Soltau points out one such reference in Ps. xlv. 8, where it is stated: "All Thy garments *smell* of myrrh, and aloes, *and* cassia . . ." Leaving out the words which are written in italics, which are not in the original, it reads: "All Thy garments of myrrh, and aloes, cassia . . ." This makes it to read as though the garments of the king were made of a composition of sweet spices, and not of material scented with them.

Another similar reference is in Ps. cix. 4 the latter clause: "but I *give myself unto* prayer". Again, leaving out the italics to get the original rendering, it is: " but I prayer ". Thus David became to his adversary—prayer. This is the sense that has to be read into the robe of the ephod. It was " made of blue ". Blue is a typical colour of

GRACE. This is a glorious truth. The High Priest may endeavour to be gracious, but Christ IS grace. " Grace and truth came by Jesus Christ " (John i. 17). The beautiful blue sky never reminds us of judgment, the storm clouds do that. The gathering blackness tends to make one fearful but the blue sky brings cheer and reminds us of the goodness of the Lord and His great grace.

Blue was the colour which abounded in both the Tabernacle and its ministry. It was in the vail, the curtains, the door, and the gate. Every piece of furniture was covered with a blue cloth when in transit. A blue lace fastened the holy crown to the head of the priest, while a lace of blue secured the breastplate of judgment to the ephod. Blue was worked into both the ephod and the curious girdle, whilst the robe was " all of blue ". As blue was in abundance in the Tabernacle, so grace is to be seen everywhere in the Church of God today. We are compelled to say with the Apostle Paul: " By the grace of God I am what I am; and His grace which was bestowed upon me was not in vain; but I laboured more abundantly than they all; yet not I, but the grace of God which was with me " (1 Cor. xv. 10). Then with Dr. Doddridge we will sing:

" Grace !—'tis a charming sound,
    Harmonious to the ear;
Heaven with the echo shall resound,
    And all the earth shall hear.

'Twas grace that wrote my name
  In God's eternal book:
'Twas grace that gave me to the Lamb,
  Who all my sorrows took.

Grace taught my wand'ring feet
  To tread the heavenly road;
And new supplies each hour I meet,
  While pressing on to God.

Grace taught my soul to pray,
  And made mine eyes o'erflow;
'Tis grace which kept me to this day,
  And will not let me go.

Grace all the work shall crown
  To everlasting days
It lays in Heaven the topmost stone
  And well deserves the praise."

This grace is something which ought to cause our souls to cry out and shout; for the righteousness of God as is depicted in that spotless coat of fine white linen is by the natural man as unattainable as the judgment of God is unapproachable for the sinner at the " Great white throne ", but God has covered the white with the blue, or He has covered law with grace. It is not our filthy rag righteousness but His own righteousness which He has imputed by His grace that gives us access to God. The foundation of His grace is His righteousness.

This robe also sets forth His

DIVINITY. It was pointed out in my last book, *Made According to Pattern*, that blue is the colour which is emblematic of divinity, while here we have been setting it forth as that which tells of His grace. This is not a confliction of thought nor yet a contradiction of truth, but it is one of the things that carries a dual meaning because nothing can embrace nor yet give expression to all that God is in Christ Jesus. As the blue vaulted heavens are immeasurable so is the Divine Son of God.

A further picture of His eternal Deity, His Divine Personage, and His matchless grace is seen in the fact that it was woven in one piece—it was seamless. This indeed was cunning work. It was the work of an artificer. But no loom on earth could ever have produced the wonderful fabric of the Incarnate God. While Christ was born of a woman and found in fashion as a man yet that did not alter His external existence. It was but a small phase of it. He was with the Father from before the foundation of the world—He was eternal. " I and My Father are one " said He on one occasion. He was Divine. As we gaze upon that example of perfect humanity we see Immanuel—God with us, or God manifest in the flesh. His life was seamless. It had no beginning, it knows no end. During the little time He tabernacled in the human flesh, it was said of Him : " Jesus knowing that the Father had given all things into His hands, and that He was come from God and went to God; He riseth from supper, and laid aside His garments . . . " (John xiii. 3-4). Thus was His eternal existence ever declared.

This robe of the ephod was not only seamless but it was made in such a way that it was not possible for man to rend it. There was a hole in the top of it through which the head passed. This hole had a neck band which, we are told, was bound to the strength of habergeon. An habergeon is an armoured plate or a coat of mail. This instruction was given to Moses by God, therefore it was in the Divine Plan.

How many would strip Jesus our Great High Priest, of His Divinity? But they could not and cannot. Every time man inflicted a doubt, saying: " *If* Thou be the Son of God " God was there to prove that He was. The Devil said: " *If* Thou be the Son of God " in Judea's wilderness, but he was vanquished with the " It is written ". While Christ was on the Cross the people said: " Let Him save Himself *if* He be Christ the chosen of God " (Luke xxiii. 35). The soldiers said: " *If* Thou be the king of the Jews save Thyself " (Luke xxiii. 37). One of the malefactors joined the cry of doubt, saying: " *If* Thou be Christ, save Thyself and us " (Luke xxiii. 39). But to all these " ifs " came the challenge of the resurrection on the third day. Man said " Is not this the carpenter's son?" (Matt. xiii. 55). God said: " This is My Beloved Son in Whom I am well pleased " (Matt. iii. 17).

It was thought that the robe of Divinity had been rent from the Lord on the day they laid Him in the tomb and set the seal upon the stone—but instead of that it was Christ calling to see the last enemy that was to be put under His feet—death—and, meeting him in his retreat, He destroyed him, and, irrespective of guard, seal and stone, He came forth again and went back into eternity, via Olivet. Thus it is that we can join with Paul and say: " O death, where is thy sting? O grave, where is thy victory? The sting of death is sin; and the strength of sin is the law. But thanks be to God, which giveth us the victory through our Lord Jesus Christ " (1 Cor. xv. 55-57).

We have said that the blue robe was an emblem of kingly grace. How many would endeavour to show us grace today in shreds, a weak and broken grace that cannot keep a man. Blessed be God, He has made grace to be unrendable! Works may fail, our love may waver, our passions may vary, but grace does not depend on these things or it would be merited and the word means "unmerited favour". The Word of God says: "For by grace are ye saved through faith; and that *not of yourselves; it is the gift of God*" (Eph. ii. 8). "For the grace of God that bringeth salvation hath appeared to all men" (Titus ii. 11). "That being justified by His grace, we should be made heirs according to the hope of eternal life" (Titus iii. 7), etc., etc.

One thing remains to be considered in regard to this garment, and that is the hem, for upon it were the only adornments. They were golden bells and pomegranates alternating all the way round.

THE POMEGRANATES. These were made of blue, purple and scarlet. They acted as pads between each of the bells thus preventing them from clashing against each other with discord. The pomegranates being a fruit most naturally suggests fruitfulness to us. We are given to understand that although the pomegranate is not over appreciated in England, yet it is considered a luscious fruit in the East. As the apple is the fruit of love (S. of S. ii) and the grape is the emblem of joy (John xv), so the pomegranate is that which speaks of peace (Joel i). Love, joy and peace go together (Gal. v. 22). Pomegranates belong to Canaan, they do not grow in the land of "leeks, onions and garlick". The two spies brought back pomegranates with their large bunch of grapes from Eshcol (Num. xiii. 23) as a witness that the land was fruitful. In that inspired Song of Solomon we read: "I went down into the garden of nuts to see the fruit of the valley, and to see whether the vine flourished, and the pomegranates budded" (vi. 11). "Let us get up early to the vineyards; let us see if the vine flourish, whether the tender grape appear, and the pomegranates bud forth; there will I give thee my loves " (vii. 12). Lovely pictures of peace and rest, but when we see this fruit on the hem of the High Priest's garment we catch a glimpse of Him, Who, with royal robe and the fruit of the Peace made by the Cross, stands as King of Peace and Righteousness, the greater than Melchisedec. He came as the Prince of Peace, He made Peace through His Cross, and now He intercedes for us who are those who have peace with God through our Lord Jesus Christ. Between the pomegranates, the fruit of peace, are the

GOLDEN BELLS which tell us of the gospel of peace. It has been remarked that there was no discord. The truth is that each bell had a distinct mellow ring, and yet they rang together with beautiful melody. That is just like the gospel of Jesus Christ. While it is was written by independent men at different times, each with his own personality and each from his local viewpoint, the individual writer rings clear and yet they ring together without jar, discord, or contradiction.

" Gospel bells, how they ring,
        Over land from sea to sea;
    Gospel bells, freely bring
        Blessed news to you and me."

The High Priest did not wear these bells on the Day of Atonement when he went into the Holiest of All with the blood, for it was a day of humiliation when he only wore plain white garments of linen. He wore the robes on every other day in the year when he ministered in the Holy place where were the golden altar of intercession, the candlestick, and the table of shewbread. It was here that his sound could be heard, for man was not permitted to enter any part of the Tabernacle except, of course, the court. Whilst the priest lived and moved the bells rang, and while the bells rang the people knew the priest was alive. We can know that Jesus lives and that He is making intercession for us for we, too, can hear the bells. Child of God, can you hear the bells now ringing? If you can, they will cheer your fainting heart. Listen! Soul in darkness, they will tell you He is your Light. Listen!! Child of sorrow and disappointment, it is a note of joy and hope. Listen!!! Tired one, do you hear the heavenly sound? Jesus lives to make intercession for *YOU.*

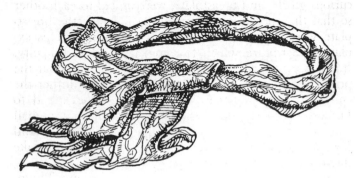

THE CURIOUS GIRDLE.

CHAPTER VI

THE EPHOD AND CURIOUS GIRDLE

Exod. xxviii. 5-8; xxxix. 1-5; *Lev.* viii. 7; 1 *Sam.* xxx. 7; *Hosea* iii. 4.

" And they shall take gold, and blue, and purple, and scarlet, and fine linen. And they shall make the ephod of gold, of blue, and of purple, of scarlet, and fine twined linen, with cunning work. It shall have the two shoulder-pieces thereof joined at the two edges thereof; and so it shall be joined together. And the curious girdle of the ephod, which is upon it, shall be the same, according to the work thereof; even of gold, of blue, and purple, and scarlet, and fine twined linen " (Exod. xxviii. 5, 8).

NOTHING is said concerning this garment and very little can be learnt from it as a garment. Its lessons are secreted in the colours. From the text we would conclude that it was made as a back and a front joined only on the shoulders by means of the shoulder stones, and made secure below by means of the curious girdle. The ephod, curious girdle, and breastplate, were united to each other so that they became inseparably one. Inside the breast-plate were deposited Urim and Thummim. This explains a Scripture which to some has held a difficulty. It is 1 Sam. xxx. 7-8: " And David said to Abiathar the priest, Ahimelech's son, I pray thee, bring me hither the ephod. And Abiathar brought thither the ephod to David. And David enquired at the Lord, saying, shall I pursue after this troop? Shall I overtake them? And He answered him, Pursue: for thou shalt surely overtake them, and without fail recover all."

David asked for the ephod to have Urim and Thummim because the Amalekites had come up against Ziklag, destroyed it, and taken David's two wives. He desired therefore to seek the mind of God as to what he should do in the matter, and it was by Urim and Thummim that God revealed His Will to him.

As to the shoulder-stones, which were onyx stones set into ouches of gold, mention will be made of them in a later chapter.

All the beauty, all the types, and all the lessons, lie enshrined in the glorious colours of this vestment which, with the addition of gold, are the same as those seen in the fabrics of the Tabernacle. Twenty-four times in the book of Exodus are these colours mentioned yet always in the same order — gold, blue, purple and scarlet, and fine twined linen. Blue and scarlet can sometimes be a clash, but purple between them harmonises each with the other. We shall not consider them strictly in their order so that we may learn the reason for their order; we shall notice later the purpose of deviation.

GOLD. This was not a tarnishing tinsel, nor yet a golden colour, but real gold. We are informed in Exod. xxxix. 3 how it was put in. " And they did beat the gold into thin plates, and cut it into wires, to work it in the blue, and in the purple, and in the scarlet, and in the fine linen, with cunning work." The gold being a metal must have stiffened the ephod as well as giving it a glory and brilliance which was unsurpassing. One can well appreciate the words: " garments . . . for glory and beauty."

Gold as we know is the emblem of Eternal Deity, that which speaks of the Godhead, because it was then the most precious metal as well as the metal that stood the test of time. There is nothing that will alter gold. It is not affected by exposure to the air and it will not deteriorate if buried for thousands of years. Acid will not destroy it, and fire will not burn it; from these it only comes out purified. " It can be beaten into leaves so exceedingly thin that one grain in weight will cover fifty-six square inches, such leaves having the thickness of only one two hundred and eighty-two thousandth part of an inch. A single grain may be drawn into a wire 500 feet long, and an ounce of gold covering a silver wire is capable of being extended upwards of 1,000 miles. It may be melted and remelted without loss by oxidation " (*The British Encyclopaedia*).

Its properties are really amazing. What a type for the great eternal Godhead, and yet it does not express Him. " To whom then will ye liken Me, or shall I be equal? saith the Holy One " (Isa. xl. 25). His is the uncreated and eternal glory, and that glory was also in His Son. " And we beheld His glory, the glory as of the only begotten of the Father " (John i. 14). The glory of the Priesthood of Christ centred in the fact that He ministered in the power of an endless life. " No man," says He, " taketh My life from Me, I have power to lay it down, I have power to take it again." See that gold dazzling in its brightness throughout His earthly life?

It shone in His immaculate Birth, its brilliance was seen on the Mount of Transfiguration; again it sparkled as He said: " Lazarus, come forth." During the dark hours of the Cross its radiancy was resplendent with glory as utterance after utterance fell from the lips that were dried and parched with suffering, ending with the words: " Father, into Thy Hands I commend My spirit " (Luke xxiii. 46). No wonder the centurion glorified God. The non-perishing gold of His Deity is wonderfully expressed by the apostle in Heb. i., particularly *vv.* 11 and 12: " They (the heavens) shall perish; but Thou remainest; and they all shall wax old as doth a garment; and as a vesture shalt Thou fold them up, and they shall be changed; but Thou art the same, and Thy years shall not fail."

BLUE is the second colour here; but the first in order in the Tabernacle where the gold was not found in the fabrics. Blue, we have asserted before, is the colour which in Scripture typifies Divinity—gold and blue side by side, Deity and Divinity together. Can anything be more glorious? Observe how these four colours, gold, blue, purple and scarlet, harmonise in nature, and in particular, the gold and the blue. Stand on the seashore towards the evening of a summer's day and watch these colours come before the vision in the beauty of nature. They will cause the colours in this garment to fade away into insignificance but, while beholding them in nature, let your soul meditate upon the God of nature. The result will be a marvelling at the beauty of the Lord our God and a confessing that " He is the altogether lovely One ".

Above is the beautiful azure *blue* sky, calm and serene; before lies the deep *blue* of the ocean. The *golden* sun is beginning to set towards the west and as it does it sends a path of *gold* across that *blue* sea, and so the first colours stand forth in their glory. As that sun sinks lower to-

wards the horizon it clothes the scattered clouds in a
livery of *scarlet,* a scene that grips one's soul. The sun is
still sinking and as it begins to disappear its rays blend
together the *blue* and the *scarlet,* which always make
purple, and so a *purple* cap is put upon the head of the
mountains and a *purple* cloak of haze is thrown around
the distant horizon. Yes! Words fail to express the
glories of nature when the Hand of God begins to move
across the sky. As we stand and behold such beauty we
are constrained to sing:

> " Holy, holy, holy, Lord God of Hosts,
>   Heaven and earth are full of Thee
>   Heaven and earth are praising Thee
>   O Lord most High."

Considering at the moment the particular colour blue,
the thoughts are directed towards Divinity or that which
speaks of Him as the Eternal Son of God. Blue is seen
in God's handiwork by gazing upwards towards the
vaults of heaven. Who can measure its expanse, or who
can tell its height? The moon is 240,000 miles away from
the earth, and the sun is ninety-three million miles away.
It is asserted that half a million stars have been counted
and that possibly three thousand million remain un-
charted. The heavens, therefore, tell of infinite space,
but Christ is infinitely greater. He was with the Father
when this solar system was brought into being. Isaiah
tells us that God " stretcheth out the heavens as a curtain,
and spreadeth them out as a tent to dwell in " (Isa. xl. 22),
whilst the writer to the Hebrews says that one day He
will take them and fold them up like a vesture, so that
the heavens and the earth will pass away, " BUT Thou
remainest."

Can anything touch, defile or pollute these heavens? Clouds may gather in the lower regions, fogs and mists may rise from the earth and so dim the vision, but the heavens remain unchangeably the same. When the clouds break and the mists have rolled away there is the blue of the heavens. What a wonderful picture of the experiences of the spiritual life. Oppression may come from the realms of Satan, while the cares of life and the problems of the world may mystify life and perhaps rob us temporarily of the joy of our salvation as they did with David, but, through them all, He is the same. Difficulties come but difficulties go. Disappointments become His appointments as we learn to trust where we cannot see and to sing:

> " Jesus never fails,
> Jesus never fails,
> Heaven and earth may pass away
> But Jesus never fails."

SCARLET. Blue and scarlet can oft-times stand in great contrast to each other, thus needing the purple as an intermediary colour to blend them. This is exactly what we have here; thus it is that we are dealing with the extremes first and explaining the third colour last. As you look upwards for the blue in Palestine or Sinai, where the record was given, you would look downwards for the red, for it is the colour of the earth. Blue and red are therefore opposites. The name Adam comes from a root word " Adham " which means " red earth ", and from this he was made. Esau was a man of the earth with carnal desires and earthly appetite, for he sold his birthright for a dish of red lentils. In the account of his birth it is said that he came out " red and hairy " (Gen. xxv. 25).

The revelation that comes through the Word of God is that He, Who had His beginning with God and Who was the Son of God (blue), stepped down from heaven to earth and became the Son of Man (red) and dwelt amongst us.   The step he made was stupendous because the dye was deeper than that of the *Adham* " red earth ", it was scarlet, a colour derived from the *coccus ilicis* or cochineal, which in Hebrew is termed " the scarlet worm " and therefore the colour is called " worm scarlet ".   When Christ humbled Himself He stepped to the very lowest.   So it was that He " Who, being in the form of God, thought it not robbery to be equal with God : But made Himself of no reputation, and took upon Him the form of a servant, and was made in the likeness of men : And being found in fashion as a man, He humbled Himself, and became obedient unto death, even the death of the Cross " (Phil. ii. 6-8)· David in his prophetic Psalm (xxii. 6) said concerning the Lord : " I am a worm and no man."

Our consideration has drawn from these two colours two extreme facts.   The one denotes Divinity and the other Humanity.   Now these have become diverse from each other because of sin, for it was sin that separated man from God.   Is it possible that there can be harmony again ?   Naturally speaking the answer is in the negative.   But when blue and scarlet are mixed they produce

PURPLE which is the intermediate colour.   Now Christ was made in the likeness of man that He might bring man back to the likeness of God.   Mystery of all mysteries, wonder of all wonders !   When blue and red, Divinity and humanity, God and man, were blended we have revealed Jesus, Immanuel — God with us — or God manifested in the flesh.   As such and only as such could He become a Mediator.   As God (blue) Jesus can satisfy the claims of God; as man (scarlet) Jesus can meet the needs of man, and as a Mediator (purple) Jesus is able to bring God and man together. " For there is one God and one Mediator between God and men, the Man·Christ Jesus " (1 Tim. ii. 5).

All these glorious colours, possessing such wonderful truths, were worked upon a background of fine twined linen, the essence of His Righteousness apart from which He never could have become a Mediator and a Priest. This is glorious truth for in the natural such a thing could never be. It is an easy thing for man to mediate between man and man. When a disagreement takes place between masterman and workmen a mediator, who is a third person, operates between them seeking a reconciliation. This is a normal state of affairs easy to arrange because all parties concerned are men. But should a difference arise between a man and an animal, a dog becoming ferocious or an ass becoming stubborn, no arbitrator can be found to conciliate because the opposing forces are different, one is human, the other animal, and there is no common ground of approach and no intermediary that can enter into the feelings and understandings of both.

Such was the position when, through sin, God and man were separated from each other in the beginning. There was none who could negotiate, mediate or arbitrate, because there was nothing common between them — God and man, Creator and creature, Divinity and humanity, Holiness and sin. It was when this impossible situation maintained that the stupendous announcement was made that: " In the fulness of time God sent forth His Son born of a woman." He, as God, could understand God, and as man He could enter into the feelings of man; and thus, as both, He was able to become the

Mediator between God and man.

THE CURIOUS GIRDLE. This girdle was neither loose nor attached but one with the ephod. " And the curious girdle of the ephod, which is upon it, shall be of the same."

The term " curious " which has been attached to the girdle seems to be very applicable for it is difficult to ascertain exactly what this girdle means. The name in its original form means " device ". A girdle is always used to strengthen the loins, thus equipping a man for a strenuous walk. " And ye shall eat it, with your loins girded, your shoes on your feet . . . " (Exod. xii. 11); or for work, as in the life of the Lord : " He riseth from supper, and laid aside His garments; and took a towel, and girded Himself " (John xiii. 4); or for warfare : " Put on the whole armour of God · . . stand therefore, having your lions girt about with truth " (Eph. vi. 11-14). When we consider the dignified position of the High Priest robed in his vestments of glory and beauty we are bound to observe that in his robes he would not go for long walks, neither would he engage in secular work, and he was certainly exempt from war. Then why did he wear this " device "? Henry Soltau says that the statement concerning the curious girdle in Lev. viii. 7 : " and bound it unto him therewith ", literally reads " and ephodised him with it, the object apparently being to convey the thought that this curious belt so connected the ephod with the person who wore it as to impart to him the virtues it contained."

Another way of expressing the thought is : " And thou shalt make a ' bind until it becomes part of ' girdle." This appears to be its intention. The robes as they have been considered speak of the character of Christ — white, His Righteousness — blue, His Divinity — scarlet, His

Humanity — purple, His Mediatorialship — bells and pomegranates, His Peace. All these things like character are inseparably bound to Him because they are part of Him. You may rob a man of his reputation (what he is thought to be) but you cannot take from a man his character because that is what he really is.

May we so be bound up in Christ that His character becomes our character because we are one with Him.

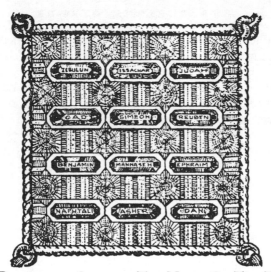

THE BREASTPLATE SHOWING THE NAMES OF THE TRIBES.

CHAPTER VII

THE BREASTPLATE OF JUDGMENT

Exod. xxviii. 9-30; *Gen.* xlix.; *Deut.* xxxiii.

" And thou shalt take two onyx stones, and grave on them the
names of the children of Israel; six of their names on one stone, and
the other six names of the rest on the other stone, according to their
birth. With the work of an engraver in stone, like the engravings
of a signet, shalt thou engrave the two stones with the names of the
children of Israel : and thou shalt make them to be set in ouches of
gold. And thou shalt put the two stones upon the shoulders of the
ephod for stones of memorial unto the children of Israel : And Aaron
shall bear their names before the Lord upon his two shoulders for
a memorial.

" And thou shalt make ouches of gold; and two chains of pure
gold at the ends; of wreathen work shalt thou make them, and fasten
the wreathen chains to the ouches.

" And thou shalt make the breastplate of judgment with cunning
work; after the work of the ephod thou shalt make it; of gold, of
blue, and of purple, and of scarlet, and of fine twined linen, shalt

thou make it. Foursquare it shall be being doubled; a span shall be the length thereof, and a span shall be the breadth thereof. And thou shalt set in it settings of stones, even four rows of stones: the first row shall be a sardius, a topaz, and a carbuncle: this shall be the first row. And the second shall be an emerald, a sapphire, and a diamond. And the third row a ligure, an agate, and an amethyst. And the fourth row a beryl, and an onyx, and a jasper: they shall be set in gold in their inclosings. And the stones shall be with the names of the children of Israel, twelve, according to their names, like the engravings of a signet; every one with his name shall they be according to the twelve tribes.

" And thou shalt make upon the breastplate chains at the ends of wreathen work of pure gold. And thou shalt make upon the breastplate two rings of gold, and shalt put the two rings on the two ends of the breastplate. And thou shalt put the two wreathen chains of gold in the two rings which are on the ends of the breast-plate. And the other two ends of the two wreathen chains thou shalt fasten in the two ouches, and put them on the shoulder-pieces of the ephod before it.

" And thou shalt make two rings of gold, and thou shalt put them upon the two ends of the breastplate in the border thereof, which is in the side of the ephod inward. And two other rings of gold thou shalt make, and shalt put them on the two sides of the ephod underneath, toward the forepart thereof, over against the other coupling thereof, above the curious girdle of the ephod. And they shall bind the breastplate by the rings thereof unto the rings of the ephod with a lace of blue, that it may be above the curious girdle of the ephod, and that the breastplate be not loosed from the ephod. And Aaron shall bear the names of the children of Israel in the breastplate of judgment upon his heart, when he goeth in unto the Holy Place, for a memorial before the Lord continually.

" And thou shalt put in the breastplate of judgment the Urim and the Thummim; and they shall be upon Aaron's heart, when he goeth in before the Lord: And Aaron shall bear the judgment of the children of Israel upon his heart before the Lord continually." (Exod. xxviii. 9-30.)

LET US bear in mind while lingering around this wonderful subject of the Breastplate that which we have already learned — the Ephod, Girdle, Shoulder-stones, and Breastplate, were all united and therefore were one; also that the same wonderful colours of the Ephod and Girdle were in the Breastplate· Thus the Breastplate is a type of the Lord Jesus Christ in His Deity, Divinity, Humanity, Mediatorialship, and Righteousness.

It was called the Breastplate of Judgment which meant " the ornament of decisions ". Its sole purpose was to be a repository for the Urim and Thummin by which God was to give His judgment or His decision in the event of doubt. On the outside were the twelve precious stones bearing the names of the twelve tribes of Israel for whom judgment was given. " And thou shalt put in the breastplate of judgment the Urim and the Thummim; and they shall be upon Aaron's heart, when he goeth in before the Lord; and Aaron shall bear the judgment of the children of Israel upon his heart before the Lord continually " (Exod. xxviii. 30).

The breastplate was doubled so as to form a pouch into which Urim and Thummim were no doubt deposited. Its shape was foursquare. There is a repetition of the word " foursquare " in the teaching of the Tabernacle. The brazen altar, the golden altar, and the Breastplate are each of them thus described. Foursquare is a geometrical figure which has equal measurements. It speaks of solidity, balance and equality. Christ's sacrificial work represented by the brazen altar is solid, reasonable and without partiality, it is the same for sinners on this side of the world or on the other. His intercessory work (the golden altar) knows no favouritism; His Priestly work is for the whole Church of the redeemed equally. Christ does not see denominationalism, and no particular sect can say that this side of the Breastplate represents them and that side does not. Whether Jew or Gentile, whether Greek or Scythian, whether bond or free, male or female, red, yellow, brown, or white, He mediates for all the same, on the one common ground that they are accepted in the Beloved through faith in the Blood.

The size is not without significance, a span foursquare. That is nine inches square which meant that it just covered the whole of the priest's breast, and as we know the breast to be a symbol of affection and love then it would tell us that the whole of His love is towards the believer. "Having loved His own which were in the world, He loved them unto the end " (John xiii· 1).

Specification is given concerning the attachments.

RINGS — CHAINS — LACES. There were six rings altogether, although only four were on the Breastplate itself, the remaining two being on the ephod just above the curious girdle as the means of securing on the ephod. The four rings of the Breastplate were placed in the four corners. From the two upper rings there proceeded wreathen chains of gold which linked the Breastplate to the shoulder-stones above, while attached to the lower rings were laces of blue fastening the Breastplate to the rings of the ephod. These chains and laces were the same two colours again, gold and blue, the gold of Deity and the blue of Grace. God above demanded Holiness and Justice. These attributes were found in Christ and so He was accepted of God, and the two golden chains linked them together. On the other hand man below needed Grace and Mercy. Christ reached down and gave them to man and so the laces of blue linked man to Christ.

This ribband of grace was later given to man to wear. The story is to be found in Num. xv. In the latter part of that chapter a man is found gathering sticks on the Sabbath day, thus breaking the commandment in Exod. xxxi. 14. The Mind of God was sought on the matter, and God said he must be put to death, again a fulfilment of Exod. xxxi. 15. The law can show no mercy, it must be adhered to rigidly. God, therefore, desirous of showing Himself merciful, said: " Speak unto the children of Israel, and bid them that they make them fringes in the borders of their garments throughout their genera-

tions, and that they put upon the fringe of the borders
a ribband of blue : And it shall be unto you for a fringe,
that ye may look upon it, and remember all the commandments of the Lord, and do them : and that ye seek
not after your own heart and your own eyes, after which
ye use to go a-whoring : That ye may remember, and do
all my commandments, and be holy unto your God "
(Num. xv. 38-49). God's mercy therefore put before their
eyes a constant reminder of the fact that He was a covenant keeping God. One is left wondering whether it was
this fringe of mercy and ribband of grace that the woman
touched when she reached out to the border of His garment (Luke viii. 44). She certainly contacted the spring
of His mercy and love so that virtue flowed forth from
Him with healing power.

THE PRECIOUS STONES. Twelve of these stones
were set into the Breastplate, each one bearing the name,
and representing one of the twelve tribes of Israel. In
seeking application for this present day, we would remind
ourselves of the glorious truth that we are spiritual Israel
born from above, so that, as Aaron bore the names of
Israel upon his breast when he went into the presence
of God, even so Jesus, our Great High Priest, bears our
names on His Heart as He stands in the presence of God
to make intercession for us.

A general survey will show us firstly that " they shall
be set in gold in their inclosings ". The Breastplate with
its multi-colours we have already noted sets forth Christ.
Gold has been commented on as that which represents
the Eternal Godhead. The picture therefore is that the
believers are set into Christ by God Himself. That indeed
is true of us for no man taketh this honour unto himself
for, said Christ : " Ye have not chosen Me, but I have
chosen you and ordained you " (John xv. 16).   Again,

"According as He hath chosen us in Him before the foundation of the world" (Eph. i. 4).

They were then set in order: God is always the God of order. It is seen everywhere in the material world, it can be seen with the same clarity in the spiritual world. The order of the stones placed in four rows of three was thus: sardius, topaz, carbuncle, emerald, sapphire, diamond, ligure, agate, amethyst, beryl, onyx, and jasper. On each stone was engraved the name of one of the twelve tribes in the following order: Judah, Issachar, Zebulun, Reuben, Simeon, Gad, Ephraim, Manasseh, Benjamin, Dan, Asher, and Naphtali.

The names on the two shoulder-stones were thus: Reuben, Simeon, Levi, Judah, Dan, and Naphtali, on the one stone; and on the other stone Gad, Asher, Issachar, Zebulun, Joseph, and Benjamin.

The names vary both as to the persons and also order. In the Breastplate the names of Levi and Joseph do not appear, but they are found on the shoulder-stones; in the Breastplate are the names of Ephraim and Manasseh, but these are absent from the shoulder-stones. The question is naturally asked, Why is this? The narrative supplies the answer. With reference to the two shoulder-stones *v.* 10 says: "Six of their names on one stone, and the other six names of the rest on the other stone *according to their birth*"; while of the Breastplate it is stated: "And the stones shall be with the names of the children of Israel, twelve, according to their names, like the engravings of a signet; every one with his name shall they be *according to the twelve tribes.*" The one was order of birth, the other order of tribe. There was a tribal order ordained by God. It is recorded in Num. x. when the children of Israel made their first move from Sinai. God has a place for every man, and He desires that every man shall be in his place. What was the reason for this specification?

(1) *As to the shoulder-stones.* The foundation of the names here, which are according to birth, is common, all twelve are written on onyx stones. So far as family relationship is concerned God, Who is no respecter of persons, sees us all the same. Every believer is seen by God " in Christ Jesus "· We are " chosen in Him ", we are " accepted in Him " (Eph. i). The common ground of our acceptance by God is redemption through the Blood of Christ. Could there be a better place for the names of those who are begotten into the family of God than on the Shoulder of the Great High Priest? Because Jesus is not only Priest, He is also the Shepherd, and it was upon His shoulder that He brought the wandering sheep back to His fold. Reuben may drop back positionally on the Breastplate while Judah might advance, but in neither case did it affect the order of birth. Even so with the Christian. God has no index to the Book of Life. The youngest convert is as much saved as the oldest saint. There are differences, of course, but these are in connection with service and reward which will now be considered.

(2) *As to the Breastplate.* The very first thing that impresses one is the variety of stones upon which the names were written. There were not two alike. Here then, with the names in tribal order, or in an order of distinction, is a picture of the Church of God on earth, with no two believers alike. It must not be overlooked that, while there was variety, there was also harmony, so that *twelve* stones made *one* Breastplate, even as *seven* branches made one candlestick. The Church is made up of many members, every one of them having his own individuality. What a variety of character! What differences of tempera-

ment!! We all look at life from various angles, our views on doctrine differ thus necessitating the many denominations. Denominationalism need not be an hindrance to the work of God on earth if only we would realise that we are all *one* Church and so show charity to each other. In the realm of politics views differ, in the world of dietics appetites vary, in social life all live differently, and in nature flowers are diverse, in hue, scent, and shape, but it can all know harmony, so why should not the Church of Christ know that oneness of spirit?

The same thing applies in ministry for God. One person, like the sardius, is fiery and eloquent in his delivery; another is quiet, gentle, and yet persuasive, and is like the soft sapphire and is just as much in the Breastplate of God's purpose. Then there is the diamond nature, the servant of God who is so brilliant and shines with so many hues and succeeds in every phase of his versatile life. These callings may be coveted by whose who may consider themselves dull, but none of us ought to look at another in any spirit of envy or jealousy, with a covetousness for their ability. The law bids us not to covet. Remember that there was only one of each stone in the Breastplate, no duplicates; so God has given many gifts, qualities, and characters to the Church, and we each must be ourself for God and not another.

Whilst there was variation in colour, brilliance, and attraction, there was one thing in whch all twelve were the same, that was they were all *precious* stones. So with you, child of God, you are precious in His sight because of what you cost Him. Ps. cxvi. 15: " Precious in the sight of the Lord is the death of His saints " reads beautifully in the literal translation. It is thus: " Precious in the eyes of Jehovah is His Death FOR His saints." That is just the reason why we are so precious to Him.

From the stones we would direct our thoughts to the names thereon. Having already discovered that there is a difference of names and order, due to one belonging to birth and the other to tribe, it is now necessary to see wherein the difference lies as to the individual. On the shoulder-stones appear the names of Levi and Joseph both of whom were, of course, born into the family. They are substituted by Ephraim and Manasseh who, being the sons of Joseph and not Jacob, have no place on the shoulder-stones. Levi is not on the Breastplate because, as a separated tribe set apart for the ministry in holy things, he was not counted with the twelve. Joseph is not on the Breastplate and yet in a sense he is. God promised to Joseph in Gen. xlviii. 22 one portion above his brethren. Therefore he received a double inheritance in the names of his two sons Ephraim and Manasseh, and so the twelve were made up again.

A further consideration of these names creates an enquiry into the totally different order from that of birth, but perhaps this cannot be well expressed as the reason why is known only to God. He proposes and He disposes. Yet a careful observation may teach us some lessons. Reuben may have lost first place because of instability (Gen. xlix. 4). Many a Christian loses joy and blessing on this point. They are not to be depended upon in the hour when most needed. They can serve God in the fair day, but are often missing in the foul day. Judah may have been placed first by God because his name means the " Praise of Jehovah " and, as will be observed later, God always puts praise foremost. Other suggestions occur to one but as we shall study these stones one by one in their order these thoughts will be gleaned as we travel.

There is one final lesson to be learned from the general

teaching and purposes of the Breastplate before turning our consideration to the separate stones. It is that on these stones were engraved the names of the twelve tribes, thus representing the whole of Israel. We, as spiritual Israel, have our names written on His Heart. Seeing that the stones were set in the Breastplate and the Breastplate was linked to the ephod with its curious girdle, it was not possible to remove one name without removing the whole glory of the robes. This was only done once a year on the great day of atonement, when the High Priest humiliated himself and, putting on the plain white garment, he took the blood first of a bullock and afterwards of the sacrificial goat and passed within the veil, at the same time putting incense on the censer; and there in the presence of God he sprinkled the blood seven times on the Mercy seat, a perfect acceptance with God, and seven times before the Ark, a perfect standing before God. Having thus presented the blood, and it having been accepted, he then came out, and addressing the congregation without, said: " Ye are clean from all your sin." Then putting on again his garments of glory and beauty he went about his daily administration.

Even so Jesus, once in the end of the age, left heaven's glory, and putting on the plain robes of humanity He stepped down to this earth for the one great purpose of going to the Cross because the great day of atonement had come but, instead of offering a bullock for Himself and a goat for the people, He offered Himself and died. After His resurrection there came the passing in beyond the veil to present the Blood. It was not the veil of the Temple for that had been rent in twain three days previously. It was the veil of the sky. The proof that He did thus pass in is seen in the two incidents recorded in John xx. In verse 17 He said to Mary: " Touch Me not for I

have not yet ascended," and in *v.* 27 He said to Thomas
a few days after: "Reach hither thy finger, and behold
My Hands: and reach hither thy hand and thrust it into
My Side." Having thus presented to the Father His
nail-pierced Hands and satisfied the claims of God, He
returned to prove His resurrection by His many appear-
ances. Then one day standing upon the Mount of Olives
in the attitude of blessing His disciples, a cloud received
Him out of their sight. He ascended again into the glory.
He went back to put on the glory that He laid aside
when He took on His humility. Having put it on He will
never remove it again. As the priest of Israel could not
remove one name from his breast without removing most
of his priestly garments, so it is quite impossible for
Christ to remove our names without removing some of
His glory. This means that it matters not what the day
nor what the difficulty, in darkness or light, in storm or
calm, in defeat or victory, He is the same; and there He
remains at the right hand of the Majesty on high making
intercession for us.

We are never forgotten nor forsaken by Him.

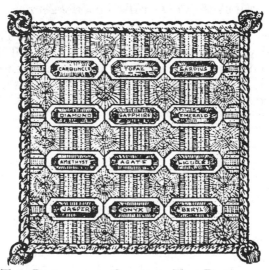

THE BREASTPLATE SHOWING THE DIFFERENT
PRECIOUS STONES.

CHAPTER VIII

INTRODUCTION TO THE PRECIOUS STONES

Gen. xxix; *Exod.* xxviii. 17-21

THE NAMES of the twelve tribes of Israel were written upon
the twelve stones of the Breastplate, every one finding
itself on a different kind of stone. A careful study will
reveal the fact that these names were not written on in
an haphazard fashion but rather that the stones were pur-
posely chosen for the engraving of the particular name.
In each case a definite connection between the character
of the person and the nature of the stone is to be seen.
Moreover, there are connections to be found between their
birth, their father's blessing, and the tribal blessing of

67

Moses. These four points in each character are the basis of the next twelve chapters. The Scriptural references will be found as follows:

1. Their Birth . . . . . . Gen. xxix. 31-xxx. 24
2. The Patriarchal Blessing . . Gen. xlix.
3. The Mosaic Blessing . . . Deut. xxx.
4. The Stones of the Breastplate . Exod. xxviii. 17-21

It would be profitable to read these references through at one sitting.

One further word of introduction might be helpful. While these men were all of them sons of Jacob, they were not all the children of one wife. Jacob had two wives, both the daughters of Laban his uncle. It was not altogether Jacob's fault that this bigamous marriage had taken place. He fell in love with Rachel and, desirous of having her as his wife, he served Laban seven years as a dowry, and said it seemed to him as only a few days. To his utter disappointment he was deceived and was given Leah, her sister. When he complained to Laban concerning his treatment Laban made the excuse that in his country the younger was never given before the older, but Laban promised to give him Rachel also seven days later if he would promise to serve seven more years for her. This he did but Rachel always remained the wife of his love, and therefore the favourite, whilst Leah was despised in his sight — yea, more than despised, for Gen. xxix 31 says she was hated. The Lord, in the same verse, seemed to recompense Leah by opening the womb while Rachel remained barren. In the East children were considered a great blessing, and sons a great inheritance. Every woman longed to be a mother, and every mother yearned for a son in the hope that her son might prove to be the promised Messiah and, if not, he continued their posterity. It was for this reason that Hannah went to the Temple and pleaded with God for a son, and God gave her Samuel.

This longing, therefore, created a rivalry between these two wives. In their desire to increase their inheritance, and either to gain favour or to retain favour in the eyes of Jacob, they both of them gave their handmaids to Jacob as concubines. It would appear that in their passion and rivalry the boys were named. This is gathered from the meanings of the various names, but behind this personal and human passion God is to be seen working His purposes out despite the human antagonism. No name was given without purpose and God's purpose at that, for every name had a meaning, and in those meanings is teaching for us, e.g. :

Reuben, which means " See a son "
Simeon, which means " Hearing "
Levi, which means " Joined "
Judah, which means " The Praise of Jehovah ".

God has sent forth Jesus, saying, See My Son, Hear ye Him, be joined to Him, and your life will be one of Praise !

So once again the old truth comes back to us that these things were written for our learning.

With this in mind let us now approach the subject of the twelve stones of the Breastplate.

CHAPTER IX

SARDIUS — JUDAH

Gen. xxix. 35; *Gen.* xlix. 8-12; *Exod.* xxviii. 17;
Deut. xxxiii. 7

" And she conceived again, and bare a son: and she said, Now will I praise the Lord: therefore she called his name Judah: and left bearing " (Gen. xxix. 35).

" Judah, thou art he whom thy brethren shall praise: thy hand shall be in the neck of thine enemies: thy father's children shall bow down before thee, Judah is a lion's whelp: from the prey, my son, thou art gone up: he stooped down, he couched as a lion, and as an old lion: who shall rouse him up? The sceptre shall not depart from Judah, nor a lawgiver from between his feet, until Shiloh come: and unto him shall the gathering of the people be. Binding his foal unto the vine, and his ass's colt unto the choice vine: he washed his garments in wine, and his clothes in the blood of grapes: His eyes shall be red with wine, and his teeth white with milk " (Gen. xlix. 8-12).

" And this is the blessing of Judah: and he said, Hear, Lord, the voice of Judah, and bring him unto his people: let his hands be sufficient for him: and be thou an help to him from his enemies " (Deut. xxxiii. 7).

HIS BIRTH. The predominant theme in this character is " Praise ". It is found in connection with his birth as well as bestowed in his blessing. It also governed his position as a tribe, and therefore, upon the Breastplate. When he was born Leah said: " Now will I praise the Lord: therefore she called his name Judah," which means " The Praise of Jehovah ". Everyone of us, like Leah, can find something for which to praise the Lord. " Praise " was evidently not only his name but his character. In all probability it was for this reason that he found himself in the leading position amongst the tribes and foremost on the Breastplate of the High Priest. God always puts praise first. This is evidenced from such Scriptures as " Whoso offereth praise glorifieth Me " (Ps. l. 23). " Enter into His gates with thanksgiving, and into His courts with praise " (Ps. c. 4). " It is good to sing praises unto our God " (Ps. cxlvii. 1), etc.

Praise will always bring blessing in its train. If you are wanting blessings from the Lord, remember they are not floating around on wings. You set up the ladder P-R-A-I-S-E from earth to heaven and down will come the blessing. The disciples were in the upper room praising the Lord when the Holy Spirit descended on the day of Pentecost. The leper, who remembered to return and thank the Lord for his deliverance, was the man who received an added blessing. Praise brings blessing, and blessing brings praise.

THE BLESSING. " *Judah, thou art he whom thy brethren shall praise.*" This man not only gave forth praise, he was also a recipient of it. Praise is infectious. We cause other people to do the same thing. There is a verse which runs:

> " Smile, smile, smile,
> For if you smile another smiles,
> And smiles come quick in piles and piles,
> And there are miles and miles of smiles
> If you smile, smile, smile."

To see the bright and right side of life is to cause someone else to see it, and they will praise God because of you.

"*Thy hand shall be in the neck of thine enemies.*" To get one's finger and thumb into the back of the neck of another means you have him subdued and conquered. He is on the ground beneath you and is unable to rise. This statement, therefore, meant victory for Judah. Every praising Christian ought to know a life of victory. While we think of our enemies, all those who would assail, and those who would seek to rise up against us, also our great arch-enemy Satan, there remains one very big enemy whom we must never forget, and that is SELF. Recognising that everything comes from God, all our powers are bestowed by Him, and praising Him daily and hourly for all that HE is to us, is surely the best way of getting the hand into the neck of self and keeping him low.

"*Thy father's children shall bow down before thee.*" Of course this meant his own brethren. The fulfilment of this phase of Judah's blessing was in fact that he became the royal tribe out of which the kings of Israel came; therefore the rest were in subjection. But there is a still fuller meaning and a deeper revelation, for out of Judah came the Messiah — the Christ — and to Him every tribe and kindred and people and tongue shall bow and confess that He is Lord of all.

"*Judah is a lion's whelp: from the prey, my son, thou art gone up; he stooped down, he couched as a lion, as an old lion: who shall rouse him up?*" Judah seems to be likened to a lion in all its phases. Firstly, as the whelp with its agile and virile life, then as the lion with its strength, and the old lion so majestic in its appearance. The statement is also a picture of a lion couching for its prey then, taking it away to the lair having feasted, lying down with a contentment and a dignity from which no one will dare to rouse him. Even so, the Christian is not a man who finds his satisfaction in that he is saved. He rejoices in his salvation, but is not content unless he brings back some trophies of grace, some prey from the forces of the enemy. Christ himself was the " Lion of the tribe of Judah ".

" *The sceptre shall not depart from Judah, nor a law-giver from between his feet until Shiloh come, and unto him shall the gathering of the people be.*" The sceptre stands as the symbol of authority and acceptance. An illustration of this is seen in the story of Queen Esther. In the fourth chapter of that book we read in *v.* 11: " All the king's servants, and the people of the king's provinces, do know, that whosoever, whether man or woman, shall come unto the king into the inner court, who is not called, there is one law of his to put him to death, except such to whom the king shall hold out the golden sceptre, that he may live." In the next chapter Esther dared to come into the presence of the king. She found favour in his sight so that he reached out the sceptre to her. When she had touched it she had the authority to ask what she would. God reaches out the sceptre which gives us the authority to go forth and preach the gospel having given to all believers the ministry of reconciliation.

Regal power meant legal power. The rod of leadership as well as the sceptre of authority belonged to, and remained, Judah's until Shiloh — the Lion of Judah's tribe — came. The coming of Christ has given to Judah a great pre-eminency, for Judah is still spoken of when many of the tribes are seldom, if ever, remembered. To have these characteristics of Judah means to have Christ dwelling within the heart in all His fulness.

" *Binding his foal unto the vine, and his ass's colt unto the choice vine; He washed his garments in wine, and his clothes in the blood of grapes. His eyes shall be red with wine and his teeth white with milk.*" Two or three lessons are to be gained from this last verse. The ass was the common beast of burden, so common practically everybody owned one, and it was used for every kind of purpose. On the other hand the vine is the type of that which is choice. It stands for fruitfulness and joy. The suggestion is, therefore, that Judah could take the common things of life and link them to the choice things, or he know how to blend the earthly and the heavenly. Not like the boy of whom it was said: " He is too heavenly minded to be of any earthly use."

The washing of his garments in wine suggests that wine was as abundant or even more abundant than water in the land of Judah, so that the choice thing became to him the common-place thing. So with the rejoicing believer, the joy of the Lord ought to enter into all the ordinary things of life, until the wine of the joy of the Lord becomes more perpetual than the water of the pleasures of the world.

The last statement made of Judah was: " His eyes shall be red with wine, and his teeth white with milk." The man of the world who suffers from inflamed eyes is the man who is addicted to intoxicating liquors. Red eyes suggest that he has been drinking wine to excess. Would to God that we would drink fuller and deeper of the wine of God's Holy Spirit, and so receive of His fulness that the joy of the Lord would radiate from our eyes. Surely this was the condition of the early disciples which caused Peter to correct a charge laid against them by saying: " For these are not drunken as ye suppose seeing it is but the third hour of the day " (Acts ii. 15).

Wine and milk are linked together. Isaiah says: " Come, buy wine and milk without money and without price " (Isa. lv. 1). Jacob says: " His eyes shall be red with wine and his teeth white with milk." Both beverages suggest strength, milk builds up the body of the child, wine masters the man, as seen in intoxication. The fruit of the vine is also the emblem of joy and we are told that " the joy of the Lord is your strength " (Neh. viii. 10).

THE MOSAIC BLESSING. Judah's position as lead-ing tribe naturally brought him great responsibilities which needed added strength. This strength was not only given to him in the symbols of wine and milk but it was requested in the blessing of Moses.

" *Hear, Lord, the voice of Judah, and bring him to his people.*" Ellicott tells how " Rashi reminds us of the many prayers in Old Testament history which were heard from Judah's lips. The prayers of David and Solomon, of Asa and Jehoshaphat, of Hezekiah against Sennacherib—and we may add of King Manasseh and Daniel the prophet — were all the ' voice of Judah '. The last line of Old Testament history is a prayer of Judah by the mouth of Nehemiah. ' Remember me, O my God, for good.' The Psalms of David, again, are all the ' voice of Judah '. And, best of all, every prayer of our Lord's is the ' voice of Judah ' also."

" *Let his hands be sufficient for him; and be Thou an help to him from his enemies.*" To those who see in this utterance a Messianic fulfilment as the Lion of the Tribe of Judah brings to perfection all that was promised to Judah, this last statement becomes obvious. A prayer to Jehovah that His Hands might be sufficient, and were they not? The Hands that ministered to the poor and needy, that touched the eyes of the blind, and brought healing to the leper. Those Hands that were presently nailed to the Cross were not only sufficient then but have been ever since, so that to-day they still minister as pierced Hands in supplication and as full Hands in continual supply.

Concerning His enemies, these have all been destroyed, including that last enemy which is Death.

> " For the Lion of Judah shall break every chain,
>   And give us the victory again and again."

THE SARDIUS. This name comes from the Hebrew word " Odem ", the root meaning of which is " red ". This, of course, was the colour of the stone. It will readily be seen that the colour of this stone was in harmony with the character whose name was indelibly inscribed thereon. Garments washed in wine and clothes in the blood of grapes mean that this rich colour flowed in abundance in his land. Then again his eyes were red with wine. What was natural in his life became the obvious in his record, or his permanent testimonial. What is predominant in life is that which will remain predominant in history.

Oh, to be ever known as one who has been washed in the Blood of the Lamb, and made precious in Him.

CHAPTER X

TOPAZ — ISSACHAR

Gen. xxx. 14-18; *Gen.* xlix. 14-15; *Exod.* xxviii. 17;
Deut. xxxiii. 18-19

" And Reuben went in the days of wheat harvest, and found mandrakes in the field, and brought them unto his mother Leah. Then Rachel said to Leah, Give me, I pray thee, of thy son's mandrakes. And she said unto her, Is it a small matter that thou hast taken my husband? And wouldest thou take away my son's mandrakes also? And Rachel said, Therefore he shall lie with thee to-night for thy son's mandrakes. And Jacob came out of the field in the evening, and Leah went out to meet him, and said, Thou must come in unto me; for surely I have hired thee with my son's mandrakes. And he lay with her that night. And God hearkened unto Leah, and she conceived, and bare Jacob the fifth son. And Leah said, God hath given me my hire, because I have given my maiden to my husband: and she called his name Issachar " (Gen. xxx. 14-18).

" Issachar is a strong ass couching down between two burdens: And he saw that rest was good, and the land that it was pleasant: and bowed his shoulder to bear, and became a servant unto tribute ' (Gen xlix. 14-15).

" And of Zebulun he said, Rejoice, Zebulun, in thy going out, and, Issachar, in thy tents. They shall call the people unto the mountain: there they shall offer sacrifices of righteousness: for they shall suck of the abundance of the seas, and of treasures laid in the sand " (Deut. xxxiii. 18-19).

HIS BIRTH. The reason for naming Leah's fifth son Issachar, which means "to hire for payment" or "reward", is discovered in the account concerning his birth. Here we have a story that is often passed by as unreadable. It is even called by some a sordid story, but surely the Bible cannot thus be discredited. If we approach the account with an honest mind we shall find that, whilst the action may not be without reproach, yet there is something there worthy of meditation. If not, we may be sure that it would never have been recorded by the Holy Spirit.

Reuben, the son of Leah, was about four or five years old. He was playing in the fields, evidently following the reapers for we are expressly told that it was at the time of the wheat harvest, when he found a pretty little red and white flower with a strong scent. Childlike he uprooted this attraction and took it home in all his innocence to his mother. The root of the mandrake is of the taproot family, various descriptions are given of it. While the child had brought the flower home to his mother, his aunt Rachel had noticed the root and had coveted it because the Eastern women believed that the mandrake contained certain medical properties, if not magical qualities, which were a cure for barrenness. We know that this condition was a great grief to Rachel, for Leah had borne four sons to Jacob and whilst Rachel had sought to obtain children through her handmaid, her sister had done the same thing with the same results. She now saw what she thought was her opportunity and so requested that the mandrakes should be given to her. Instead she received the rebuff of her sister who said: "Is it a small matter that thou hast taken my husband? and wouldest thou take away my son's mandrakes also?" The result of this was that they struck a bargain with each other, which seems so peculiarly strange to us because the circumstances are foreign to us. The outcome was that Rachel secured her mandrake, but Leah was given another son. It was because of this bargaining over a mandrake that Leah named the child Issachar — " hire " or " reward ". Rachel remained barren for another two years.

THE PATRIARCHAL BLESSING. " Issachar is a strong ass couching down between two burdens." This blessing has oft-times been misinterpreted because the ass is so often considered a silly animal, but this is not true. The idea has originally come from legend and not from fact. The animal may be stubborn at times but never silly. Of the 143 references in the Scriptures not one of them would justify this characteristic, but many would prove the contrary. Balaam's ass saw the angel and sought to avoid him whilst Balaam remained blind to the situation. The ass was certainly wiser than Israel in the estimation of Isaiah when he said : " The ox knoweth his owner, and the ass his master's crib : but Israel doth not know, my people doth not consider " (Isa. i. 3). Here, too, in Issachar we shall see that same wisdom caused him to work in anticipation of the crib and for the rest which he saw was good.

The couching down between two burdens has suggested indolence and stubbornness to some minds, but this is far from the truth. If we compare Scripture with Scripture, as we are exhorted to do, instead of isolating Scripture as we are inclined to do, we would discover that the history of this tribe was the reverse of indolence. Issachar was prepared to work because of the rest at the end of the day. It is the statement " couching between two burdens " that now needs to be defined. These words have been translated in many ways as " between the cattle-pens ", between two hearth stones ", " lying down between the folds ", " within their own boundaries ". If we link the name of Issachar with that of Zebulun, as Moses did, it might be seen that God distributes men according to their ability and qualification. Zebulun was a man and a tribe with a desire for travel, a going out and a coming in, so God gave him coast lines. Issachar found his delight and pleasure in his local environment, and in his tents. He delighted to remain within his own boundaries, not to laze but to bend his back to labour. God gave to this man some of the most fertile land in Palestine. One tribe was nautical, the other agricultural. So each followed their own pursuits with equal success. How often men long to be in different circumstances or have different service, but, remember, God has put us into the most favourable circumstances, if we would but bend to them.

The incentive to solid service, to burden bearing, to progressive production, was that at the end there was rest and reward. His name meant " hire " or " reward ". His character was to give himself to hire that he might afterwards enjoy his reward. The person who can really sit down and conscientiously enjoy rest is the one who has laboured faithfully and earned it — the harder the day's work, the sweeter the evening's rest; the more weary the body, the more comfortable the bed. With this in mind we find the Apostle saying to us: " There remaineth therefore a rest to the people of God. For he that is entered into his rest, he also hath ceased from his own works, as God did from His. Let us labour therefore to enter into that rest . . . " (Heb. iv. 9-11).

Here is a glorious challenge. To enjoy heaven we must labour on earth. This, of course, has nothing to do with salvation because that is " not of works lest any man should boast ". This refers to the service of the saint.

THE MOSAIC BLESSING. Not much can be said

in addition, for we find Moses supporting the sentiments of Jacob, except to emphasise a thought already expressed which Moses brings to us by linking the two names under one joint blessing — brethren with opposite outlooks and diverse natures can labour together for God. One thinks of the opposites in the rugged, denouncing Elijah and the quiet, domestic Elisha; the temperamental Peter and the steady John; the aged Paul and his son in the faith, Timothy; and many other partners in service.

If we apply the thought to the Church then we should see the missionary enterprise of Zebulun linked with the hard plodding work of those who never leave their local Church but upon whom, through loyalty and devotion, one can always rely. To quote from the late Dr. J. Orton: " It is owing to God's directing the inclinations of men, that some are found in the country and some in the town; that some love the noise and bustle of cities and seaports, the fatigue and hazard of navigation and travelling; while others prefer the retiredness and silence of the country. Some choose to dwell with Zebulun at the haven of ships; others with Issachar in the tents of the country, among the bleatings of the flocks. Nor is this different choice entirely owing to education and habit, since it is frequently seen that young people choose a different occupation from their father, and some are uneasy till they have changed that to which they were brought up. This diversity of inclination is by appointment and influence of God, the Supreme Sovereign of every community."

THE TOPAZ. Although this stone is often mentioned in the Scriptures its origin and meaning are not easily ascertained. There is one record which tells us " that ' Topaz ' comes from a Greek word meaning ' to seek '. The stone was first found on an island in the Red

Sea which was often surrounded by fog.   And because the sailors had to seek long for the island ere they found it, they called the gem ' topaz '. "   The topaz seems from this story to be a reward for diligent seeking.   That is exactly the meaning of the name written thereon — Issachar, " a reward ".   The stone is a cheerful, golden yellow, and is said to bring beauty, wisdom and long life.   These attributes at any rate belonged to Issachar.

All Christians, like the topaz, should be bright and cheerful, reflecting the glory of their Lord.

CHAPTER XI

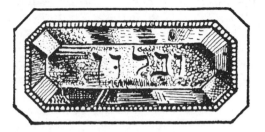

CARBUNCLE — ZEBULUN

Gen. xxx. 19-20; *Gen.* xlix. 13; *Deut.* xxxiii. 18-19

" And Leah conceived again, and bare Jacob the sixth son. And Leah said, God hath endued me with a good dowry; now will my husband dwell with me, because I have borne him six sons; and she called his name Zebulun " (Gen. xxx. 19-20).

" Zebulun shall dwell at the haven of the sea; and he shall be for an haven of ships; and his border shall be unto Zidon " (Gen. xlix. 13).

" And of Zebulun he said, Rejoice, Zebulun, in thy going out; and, Issachar, in thy tents. They shall call the people unto the mountain; there they shall offer sacrifices of righteousness; for they shall suck of the abundance of the seas, and of treasures hid in the sand " (Deut. xxxiii. 18-19).

HIS BIRTH. Not much can be said concerning the birth of this son except that, whilst he was the fifth to receive the blessing of Jacob, he was the sixth son of Leah. For some reason Jacob chose to reverse the names of Issachar and Zebulun as he reversed the order of Manasseh and Ephraim. Maybe it was because Zebulun was a more progressive man than the placid Issachar.

When Leah gave birth to this her sixth son she was

still fighting her battle for recognition and equality, for said she: "God hath endued me with a good dowry, now will my husband dwell with me, because I have borne him six sons and she called his name Zebulun," which means "dwelling". Again, behind the naming of this child is the prophetic, or perhaps the foreseeing eye of God. Both Jacob and Moses played on the meaning of his name in the bestowing of their blessings.

THE PATRIARCHAL BLESSING. "Zebulun shall dwell at the haven of the sea." We are not quite certain of the boundaries of Zebulun. It is known that one side was marked by the western shores of the Sea of Galilee, but how far the territory extended towards the Mediterranean is questionable. From these blessings it would appear that Zebulun occupied some of the main coast line although our maps do not show it thus. The ships referred to would hardly be the small boats of Galilee's lake for from an inland water one could not "suck of the abundance of the sea" neither would there be much "going out". Josephus, the historian, suggests that this land stretched from sea to sea. He says, "The tribe of Zebulun's lot included the land which lay as far as Gennesaret (Galilee) and that which belonged to Carmel and the sea." Jacob said: "And his border shall be unto Zidon."

The land of Galilee in the New Testament embraced the territories of Issachar, Zebulun, and Naphtali. This is interesting because two disciples once came to Jesus and said: "Rabbi, where dwellest Thou?" He said: "Come and see," and if we go to see where that dwelling place was it will be found to be in Zebulun. Jesus was born in Bethlehem of Judah. He dwelled in Nazareth of Zebulun. We shall come back to this dwelling. Look next at the

MOSAIC BLESSING. Moses united the blessings of Zebulun and Issachar. We shall separate them for a close study. " *Rejoice, Zebulun, in thy going out . . . they shall call the people unto the mountains . . . they shall suck of the abundance of the seas."* There are two ways in which this going out and coming in can be effected in the maritime world. This Mosaic blessing tells of the first. The going out would be with precious cargoes of merchandise, gold, wool, wines, brass, lace, and cedar, in exchange for which they would bring in the abundance of other things carried upon the seas. In this Zebulun could truly rejoice. Since then from Zebulun, known to us now as Galilee, have there gone forth the stories of Bethlehem, Capernaum, Bethsaida, Cana, and of Galilee, stories that have enriched the world, stories that have brought in an abundance from the seas, as the hearts of men have been drawn to the mountains that are round about Jerusalem, the Mount of the Beatitudes, the Mount of Transfiguration, the Mount of Olives, and last but by no means least the little Mount called Calvary. Yes, indeed, Zebulun may well rejoice. The second means of sucking of " the abundance of the seas " is made manifest in

THE CARBUNCLE, the stone of the Breastplate upon which was indelibly inscribed the name of Zebulun. The Hebrew word for Carbuncle is " Bareqeth " meaning " glittering ", and it is evidently derived from a Hebrew root used sometimes for " lightning " or " flashing ". This suggests that Zebulun, who was to " dwell at the haven of the sea " to be " an haven for ships ", might well be represented as a lighthouse with its flashing light " going out " warning the mariner of dangers, or welcoming the storm-tossed traveller to seek the refuge of the haven. Moreover, this was not only an haven for anchorage, it was an " haven for ships "; literally " And he, to, at, or on a shore for ships " which means there were docking facilities for the lading and unlading of vessels which desired to berth.

What a need there is for a welcome beam to invite the weary, worn, tear-stained traveller of this storm-tossed world to an haven of rest, not just to hide from the storm, but where men and women may unload their troubles, pour out their sorrows, discharge their sin, and find relief from their difficulties, problems, trials, and setbacks, and then to be reladen with joy and peace, and an assurance which comes through believing. We say what a need there is! Nay, that need has already been provided for if man would but see the Light and follow its beam. And Zebulun did certainly become that shore from which that Light shone and still shines. Read the words written by Isaiah (Isa. ix. 1) and confirmed by Matthew concerning Jesus (Matt. iv. 13-16): " And leaving Nazareth He came and dwelt in Capernaum, which is upon the sea coast, in the borders of Zabulon and Nephthalim. That it might be fulfilled which was spoken by Esaias the prophet, saying, The land of Zabulon and the land of Nephthalim, by the way of the sea, beyond Jordan, Galilee of the Gentiles; The people which sat in darkness saw great light; and to them which sat in the region and shadow of death light is sprung up."

Shall we become the lighthouse keepers and keep our reflectors polished and see that the beam is ever radiating, and shall we become the harbourmasters and welcome, comfort and support all who seek the refuge of the Church of God and Jesus, its Lord, and to suck in " of the abundance of the seas?"

CHAPTER XII

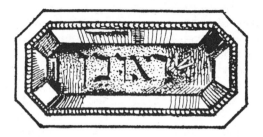

EMERALD — REUBEN

Gen. xxix. 32; *Gen.* xlix. 3-4; *Exod.* xxviii. 8;
Deut. xxxiii. 6

" And Leah conceived, and bare a son, and she called his name
Reuben; for she said, Surely the Lord hath looked upon my affliction;
now therefore my husband will love me " (Gen. xxix. 32).

" Reuben, thou art my firstborn, my might and the beginning of
my strength, the excellency of dignity, and the excellency of power:
Unstable as water, thou shalt not excel; because thou wentest up to
thy father's bed, then defiledst thou it: he went up to my couch "
(Gen. xlix. 3-4).

" Let Reuben live and not die; and let not his men be few "
(Deut. xxxiii. 6).

HIS BIRTH. There was a strong feeling between
Rachel and Leah because of a favouritism shown by
Jacob who loved Rachel and hated Leah. God, Who does
not approve of this condition of living, seemed to inter-
vene. In the East children were considered a great blessing; future posterity was everything, and to be without
a son to perpetuate the name of his father was almost
like having a curse resting upon one's head. Which of

the two was going to honour Jacob with a son? Jacob, no doubt, would have chosen to receive this blessing from Rachel his favourite, but from the text of Scripture this was where God stepped in, for we read: " And when the Lord saw that Leah was hated, He opened her womb; but Rachel was barren. And Leah conceived and bare a son " (Gen. xxix. 31-32). So overjoyed was this poor despised woman that she broke forth in rejoicing, and said: " Surely the Lord hath looked upon my affliction; now therefore my husband will love me." Thus it was that this first son came to be named Reuben for it means: " See a son." To her husband, to Rachel, to her friends and neighbours, to all who knew her, yes, even to succeeding generations she said " See a son ". This became her great hope of emancipation, she might at any rate find an equality with Rachel if not a pre-eminence over her — see a son, in him is the blessing of Jacob, for his family will continue! Does it not remind us of the cry of Isaiah the prophet who said: " Unto us a child is born, unto us a Son is given." When we were oppressed because of sin, when we were alienated from God, the Son of God came to bring us joy and salvation. Well might we say: " The Lord hath looked upon our afflictions," and then looking away to Jesus our Saviour, say: " See a Son."

The possibility is that Jacob would have refrained from giving to this child the blessing of the firstborn but for the fact that there must have been an overruling of God, for later, when God gave to Moses the law which was to control the lives of the people and the life of the nation, He very clearly revealed His Mind in such a matter as He said: " If a man have two wives, one beloved and another hated, and they have borne him children, both the beloved and the hated, and if the firstborn son be

her's that was hated: Then it shall be, when he maketh
his sons to inherit that which he hath, that he may not
make the son of the beloved firstborn before the son of
the hated, which is indeed the firstborn: But he shall
acknowledge the son of the hated for the firstborn, by
giving him a double portion of all that he hath: for he is
the beginning of his strength; the right of the firstborn is
his " (Deut. xxi. 15-17). Jacob certainly acknowledged him
as the beginning of his strength, although he did not give
him the firstborn's blessing. This was not a shortcoming
on Jacob's part but a loss sustained by Reuben himself for
he robbed himself, through his sin, of both birthright and
blessing, and these were given to the sons of Joseph and
to Judah respectively. This we learn from 1 Chron. v.
1-2: " Reuben the firstborn of Israel (for he was the firstborn: but, forasmuch as he defiled his father's bed, his
birthright was given unto the sons of Joseph, the son of
Israel: and the genealogy, is not to be reckoned after
the birthright. For Judah prevailed above his brethren,
and of him came the chief ruler; but the birthright was
Joseph's) ".

THE PATRIARCHAL BLESSING. " My firstborn."
As such he was entitled to a double blessing. E. Bendor
Samuel, quoting from the Ancient Jerusalem Targum,
relates that this blessing is thus paraphrased: " Reuben,
my firstborn art thou, my strength, and the beginning
of my sorrow. To thee, my son Reuben, would it have
pertained to receive three portions above thy brothers,
the priesthood, birthright, and kingdom, but because thou
hast sinned, the birthright is given to Joseph, the kingdom to Judah, and the High Priesthood to Levi." This
makes a treble blessing of it.

Thus we learn that whatever may be our rights and in-
heritances, sin, yea one sin, can deprive us of all. With

all his loss his sonship remained. To such a condition the apostle refers when he says: " Saved, though as by fire." It was this firstborn blessing that caused Elisha to ask of Elijah " a double portion of his spirit ".

" *My might and the beginning of my strength.*" Jacob proceeded to make known the qualities of a firstborn son such as Reuben should have had, that he and all others might know what he lost through his sin. How proud had been the parents when Reuben was born, so excited to " see a son ". " This," said Jacob, " was the beginning of my strength " — that is, of the strength of that family that was to increase in succeeding generations, but Jacob had hoped for strength of character as well as numerical strength, but in this son he had been bitterly disappointed. May we remember that as sons of God, the Lord looks for character in us. Let us not fail Him through sin.

" *The excellency of dignity and the excellency of power.*" This may have had reference to the dignity of the offices that he could have held and the power that he could have exercised therein; or it may refer to some qualities of character which he did possess but, alas, did not develop to our knowledge. These qualities are to be seen when in Gen. xxxvii. 21 he withstood his brethren for the safety of Joseph and was instrumental in saving the lad's life, although he identified himself with them in their deceit.

Again, when Joseph in Egypt demanded the bringing of Benjamin, it was Reuben who stood security to his father for his youngest brother, but he could not be relied upon — instability was his weakness — with all these privileges and qualities yet " unstable as water, thou shalt not excel ". The old man then proceeded to remind him of a vile crime he had committed some forty years earlier, the stain of which had never been removed. We need not enlarge on his sin. It would be to no profit. Sufficient to say that it is recorded in Gen. xxxv. 22. Undoubtedly the lesson God would have us learn from such a loathsome record is that, if a man is not capable of controlling his own passions, bringing his own carnal desires under strict discipline, he is certainly not capable of holding any holy office where he is responsible for controlling the lives and conduct of other people. Oh, the subtlety of sin! Truly the heart is deceitful above all things and desperately wicked.

THE MOSAIC BLESSING. "Let Reuben live and not die; and let not his men be few." This came more in the form of a request or a prayer. Reuben had lost his position, may he not lose his life and may he not lose his existence as a tribe! Surely another Old Testament picture of Grace, which is so much greater than law. There are some who think the rendering should be: "Let Reuben live and not die, *though* his men be few," which means, though he must not expect to flourish, yet let him not perish. This would reveal the limitation of Grace under the Old Testament law and thus magnify the Grace that came by Christ Jesus in the New Testament, in the which our sins are remembered against us no more.

THE EMERALD. Reuben found his name inscribed upon a precious stone like the rest, a faltering man but none the less precious. The emerald, we are told, is sea green in colour. How significant that Reuben of all names should be on it. The man who was as unstable as water found his name on a stone of the colour of the ever rolling, restless sea. Instability, and yet on the Breastplate — surely "saved, though as by fire". The Lord deliver us from being a Reuben.

CHAPTER XIII

SAPPHIRE — SIMEON

Gen. xxix. 33; *Gen.* xlix. 5-7; *Exod.* xxviii. 18

" And she conceived again, and bare a son; and said, Because the Lord hath heard that I was hated, he hath therefore given me this son also; and she called his name Simeon " (Gen. xxix. 33).

" Simeon and Levi a~ brethren; instruments of cruelty are in their habitations. O my soul, come not thou into their secret; unto their assembly, mine honour, be not thou united : for in their anger they slew a man, and in their selfwill they digged down a wall. Cursed be their anger, for it was fierce; and their wrath for it was cruel : I will divide them in Jacob, and scatter them in Israel " (Gen. xlix. 5-7).

HIS BIRTH. Simeon was the second son of Leah. When Reuben, the firstborn, arrived Leah rejoiced in the hope that her son would be the means of drawing her husband's love towards her, but seemingly this did not happen. Now that a second son was born her hopes rose once more. This time she said : " Because the Lord hath heard that I was hated (not loved, the word ' hated ' is a negative rather than a positive word), He hath therefore given me this son also." So it was she named him

92

Simeon, which means " hearing ". So must Leah have often prayed in her distress that the Lord would hear her petition and grant her that relationship, and it was these prayers she now acknowledged the Lord to be answering.

Leah brought two senses into operation in the naming of her first two sons — the eye and the ear, " seeing " and " hearing ". There was something prophetic about the naming of these children as well as something historic, the first " See a son ", the second " hearing ". Surely the human race, in all its distress created by a lack of love, is called upon to look away to Jesus and in Him to " See a Son " and then, seeing Him as the Son of God, to hear Him as the " Word of God ". That Word which was made flesh and dwelt amongst us must ever receive our listening ear. A voice from the clouds on the Mount of Transfiguration said to the disciples : " This is My beloved Son in whom I am well pleased; hear ye Him " (Matt. xvii. 5). Not only are we to engage eye and ear in attending to the Lord, but there are many passages of Scripture which reveal that His eyes and ears are ever open towards us. " The *eyes* of the Lord are upon the righteous, and His *ears* are open unto their cry " (Ps. xxxiv. 15). " And the Lord said, I have surely *seen* the affliction of My people which are in Egypt, and have *heard* their cry " (Exod. iii. 7 and Acts vii. 34). " Because the Lord hath heard," said Leah. How wonderfully true! The Lord is always ready to hear us when we talk to Him and desires that we should ever be ready to listen when He speaks to us.

THE PATRIARCHAL BLESSING. Although Simeon is being considered in this chapter and Levi in a later, yet here the two characters cannot be separated because they were one in their very stubborn and self-willed action, and they were one in the reproof that fell from the lips of their dying father.

"*Simeon and Levi are brethren*" not only because of the same parentage but they were brethren in spirit, in purpose, in character, in many things. It is a fact that similar characters will find each other out and unite themselves. The world gives expression to this fact in its proverb: " Birds of a feather flock together "; whilst the Scriptures bear out the same evidence in the Proverb: " He also that is slothful in his work is brother to him that is a great waster " (Prov. xviii. 9). This is something which speaks to each of us in very loud words saying that it is important to watch our company.

"*Instruments of cruelty are in their habitation.*" The incident referred to by Jacob is found recorded in the thirty-fourth chapter of Genesis, and can be there read for the details. It will be sufficient here to quote two short extracts to see why Jacob should at this time raise the matter. Gen. xxxiv. 25-26 sums up the crime. " And it came to pass on the third day, when they were sore, that two of the sons of Jacob, Simeon and Levi, Dinah's brethren, took each man his sword, and came upon the city boldly, and slew all the males. And they slew Hamor and Shechem his son with the edge of the sword, and took Dinah out of Shechem's house and went out." Verse 30 tells us of Jacob's immediate reaction: " And Jacob said to Simeon and Levi, Ye have troubled me to make me to stink among the inhabitants of the land, among the Canaanites and the Perizzites; and I being few in number, they shall gather themselves together against me and slay me; and I shall be destroyed, I and my house." The mercy of God prevented this feared tragedy from falling upon the house of Jacob. This crime had been committed some years before the time we are considering, yet Jacob never seemed to have survived the shock, and now on his death-bed he sought to assure all that he never approved their action. He put the responsibility upon the shoulders of them to whom it belonged, and thereby vindicated his name and that of his family.

The " instruments of cruelty " refers to their evil plan-ning to ensnare and trap, to deceive and destroy. There-fore Jacob addressed himself saying: " O my soul, come not thou into their secret; unto their assembly, mine honour, be not thou united." It is necessary sometimes for a man to be at variance against his father or a father against his sons. A servant of God must never condone with sin because it is a member of the family who has committed it. This was what brought tragedy to Eli. He failed to correct the sins of his sons. Within the family of Jesus Christ, within the circle of the Church, is found at times the element of deceitful planning which needs to be suppressed and denounced, things in which the true soul can have neither part nor parcel.

" *For in their anger they slew a man and in their self-will they digged down a wall. Cursed be their anger, for it was fierce; and their wrath, for it was cruel.*" Anger can be righteous and indignation justifiable, but they can quickly deteriorate into something very sinful. True it was that Shechem had wronged their sister, and natural it was that, as brethren, they should defend their sister and seek retribution for the evil committed against her; but the judgment is that their anger was fierce and their wrath cruel, and surely nothing justifies cruelty. In this their display of anger Jacob used the strange expression " they slew a man and digged down a wall ", and one one might look long in Gen. xxxiv for this action. Literally it is, " In their anger they slew man ", the word

" man " here being a collective singular word which means " men ".   One man had sinned against Dinah but, instead of punishing that man or even extending it to that man's family, these two brethren took each a sword and, at a time when the men of the city of Shechem were at a disadvantage, they went forth and slew every one of them. Moreover, in their stubborn cruel self-will said Jacob: " they digged down a wall." This is a very strange translation, but all commentators are agreed that the literal rendering is " they houghed ox ", or " they have ham-strung oxen ". It refers " to a process of wantonly cutting the tendons of oxen so as to make them useless ".   Ruthless cruelty to animals or to mankind is indeed an unpardonable crime, and so it was that Jacob found it necessary to remind these men of their wickedness and in telling them of their future he said: *" I will divide them in Jacob, and scatter them in Israel."* Future history shows this to have been fulfilled for, referring only to Simeon here (although it applies similarly to Levi), at the first census taken of Israel the tribe of Simeon numbered 59,300 (Num. i. 23). At a second census some years later they had been reduced to 22,300 (Num. xxvi. 14), which means that just before the conquest of the Promised Land Simeon was the smallest tribe. So much so that, whilst in each of these characters we are considering

THE MOSAIC BLESSING bestowed on each of the tribes in Deut. xxxiii, we are left to discover that Simeon is not mentioned by Moses at all. One thing must here be recorded — although Jacob laid a curse on their sin, he did not curse the sinners. These men reaped what they sowed, yet the mercy of God brought them at last to a place of honour. Let us learn that God who said: " In blessing I will bless thee," also said: " Blessed are the merciful for they shall *obtain* mercy." God's promised blessings do not mean immunity from punishment for any who transgress the commandments of God. Finally,

THE SAPPHIRE. The English word Sapphire is evidently taken from the Hebrew " Sappeer " which is derived from a verb signifying " to scratch or polish ", and also means " to cut off or divide ". It is the second hardest stone in the world. This is very interesting because Simeon's name was inscribed on the Sapphire and thus it became the foundation for his name. Do you observe the significance of this? The character of Simeon, and also of Levi, was one which was very hard, and the action against the Shechemites was one that might readily be called merciless " scratching " or tearing to pieces of a community. The result of this conduct was that they were divided in Jacob and scattered in Israel which harmonises with the derivaton of " Sapphire ", " to cut off or divide ".

CHAPTER XIV

DIAMOND — GAD

Gen. xxx. 9-11; *Gen.* xlix. 19; *Exod.* xxviii. 18;
Deut. xxxiii. 20-21

" When Leah saw that she had left bearing, she took Zilpah her maid, and gave her Jacob to wife. And Zilpah Leah's maid bare Jacob a son. And Leah said, A troop cometh; and she called his name Gad " (Gen. xxx. 9-11).

" Gad, a troop shall overcome him; but he shall overcome at the last " (Gen. xlix. 19).

" And of Gad he said, Blessed be he that enlargeth Gad: he dwelleth as a lion, and teareth the arm with the crown of the head. And he provided the first part for himself, because there, in a portion of the lawgiver, was he seated, and he came with the heads of the people, he executed the justice of the Lord, and His judgements with Israel " (Deut. xxxiii. 20-21).

HIS BIRTH. Leah had given birth to four sons, after which Rachel had made use of her handmaid in the hope of securing a son by proxy. As she had been successful Leah did the same thing, and so a child was born of Zilpah and was taken by Leah as her adopted son, she naming him Gad, which means: " A troop ", for this was her fifth son and she still longed for more, hence she made the remark: " A troop cometh." It will be sufficient to content ourselves with this brief remark concerning his birth as the rest of our chapter intertwines around this term " A troop ".

THE PATRIARCHAL BLESSING. " *Gad, a troop shall overcome him, but he shall overcome at the last.*" It is not the purpose of this work to go into the history of the tribe which shows how amazingly they fulfilled this prophetic utterance. It is ours to remain devotional and not historical. For any interested, a study of the records of the tribe of Gad will reveal them as great warriors fighting many battles, knowing both defeat and victories, showing the great prowess of a tribe of " valiant men, men able to bear buckler and sword, and to shoot with bow, and skilful in war " (1 Chron. v. 18). Is this not a great thought worthy of much consideration : " A troop shall overcome him, but he shall overcome at the last." Another way of expressing this is " stooping to conquer ". Three pictures of this truth are

(1) *Concerning Israel.* Israel was a troop. God promised to Abraham that his seed should be as numberless as the sand of the seashore and as countless as the stars of heaven, and that through his seed all the families of the earth should be blessed. The multiplication commenced in Jacob and his twelve sons, and continued until the family became a nation. Said Jacob on one occasion : " With my staff I passed over this Jordan (meaning a lonely man) and now I am become two bands (the same word, troop)," but Israel was to be overcome and then to rise. Oppressed by an " Egyptian troop " they came forth victors; overcome by a " Babylon troop " they came out of their seventy years of captivity. To-day that nation is overcome, buried in the graveyard of the nations, it has no king, no government, no home. It knows only great persecution and appalling massacres, overcome indeed by

the vile Nazi atrocities, BUT " he shall overcome at the last ". So they will ultimately come through as revealed in Ezek. xxxvii. They shall return to their land so that, when they see and recognise Him Whom they pierced, a nation shall be born in a day. Then they shall be the leading power in the world again.*

(2) *Concerning Christ.* It is declared concerning Him that every knee shall bow and every tongue shall confess Him as Lord and, in another place, that around Him will gather a company that no man can number — surely a great troop. But there was a time when it appeared that man had overcome Him as He was led by them to the Cross, and that death had gained the victory as they laid Him in the tomb, but the third day He proved that He overcame at the last as He rose triumphant. Presently we shall see Him coming forth with all the armies of heaven and with ten thousands of His saints to destroy those nations who are seeking to oppress and to overcome Him. " He shall overcome at the last."

(3) *Concerning Believers.* The Church is a troop of believers. At the moment we are pressed down by the burdens of this present life. The god of this world is having his way so that it appears as though the Church has been overcome, but we shall overcome at the last. We shall be part of the victorious troop that will sing the praises of the Lord in eternity. We shall reign with Him. Thus the great lessons are — every believer who would be an overcomer must first be overcome himself. We must be vanquished if we would be victor. Lives conquered by the grace of God become conquerors through the grace of God.

---

* In what a striking manner is this Scripture again being fulfilled before our very eyes, by the setting up of Israel as a State, following upon the World War!

THE MOSAIC BLESSING. The whole of this blessing continues to reveal the warlike nature of Gad, the tribe that delighted to be in the front of the battle; a plundering tribe always seeking to enlarge his territory and his possessions. But, said Moses:

"*Blessed be he that enlargeth Gad.*" Territorial gains and increased prosperity achieved through conflict are really possessed because of the blessing of God. We may enter into spiritual conflict, we may bring all we have to bear upon our adversary, we may plunder and ravage the citadels of Satan, yet success will be missing unless the Hand of the Lord is upon us in blessing. Like a lion, unafraid, Gad used the arm of his strength to tear in pieces the enemy, and then used the crown of the head in ruling him. Two very fine examples of the qualities of this tribe, which reveal something of the force of this Mosaic blessing, are Jephthah and Elijah, both Gadites. Jephthah, although cast out and overcome by his own people because of his unfortunate birth, rose up to deliver his people out of the hand of the Ammonites, and then "executed the justice of the Lord" as one of the judges of Israel. The other, Elijah, the rough and rugged Tishbite, the man of the wilderness, who tore to pieces the evils of Ahab and the idolatrous Baal worship, also "executed the justice of the Lord".

"*And he provided the first part for himself.*" This may be readily understood when we call to mind that, at the time of the conquest of Canaan, Gad was one of the tribes who, with Reuben and half the tribe of Manasseh, asked for their possessions straight away, telling Joshua that they would prefer to remain on the East side of Jordan. Joshua assured them that they could have the possession, providing they went forward over Jordan with their brethren and fought with them until the whole land was subdued and then they could return. To this they gave their immediate consent; so having " provided the first part for himself " they went forward to help others. Seeing that no man liveth unto himself, there is no blessing nor possession which we personally enjoy that someone else has not helped us to attain; therefore we must not " settle on our lees " whilst our fellowman needs an helping hand.

THE DIAMOND. What better stone could have been chosen on which to inscribe the name of such a character? Diamond, in our English Lexicon, is the same word as " adamant ", and adamant means " impenetrable hardness ", hardness that cannot be broken. Diamond in our Bible, according to Robertson, is derived from the Hebrew root signifying " to break in pieces or bruise ", a stone which breaks or scratches all others. As we know, the diamond is so hard that it can cut glass or precious stones. It can scratch indelible marks without hurting itself. This was true of Gad. God said to Ezekiel on one occasion " As an adamant harder than flint have I made thy forehead; fear them not, neither be dismayed at their looks, though they be a rebellious house " (Ezek. iii. 9). May the Lord give us this tenacity of purpose. The diamond is not only hard, it is precious. The Lord grant us that courage which is so precious in these days of apathy; that loyalty, the preciousness of which stands out amidst the faithlessness of our generation; that love and faith which are more precious than much fine gold; and that wisdom which in price is far above rubies.

Lord, make me a warrior !

CHAPTER XV

LIGURE — EPHRAIM

Gen. xli. 50-52; *Gen.* xlviii. 17-20; *Exod.* xxviii. 19;
Deut. xxxiii. 17

" And the name of the second called he Ephraim: For God hath caused me to be fruitful in the land of my affliction " (Gen. xli. 52).

" And when Joseph saw that his father laid his right hand upon the head of Ephraim, it displeased him: and he held up his father's hand, to remove it from Ephraim's head unto Manasseh's head. And Joseph said unto his father, Not so, my father: for this is the first-born; put thy right hand upon his head. And his father refused, and said, I know it, my son, I know it: He also shall become a people, and he also shall be great: but truly his younger brother shall be greater than he, and his seed shall become a multitude of nations. And he blessed them that day, saying, In thee shall Israel bless, saying, God make thee as Ephraim and as Manasseh: and he set Ephraim before Manasseh " (Gen. xlviii. 17-20).

" His glory is like the firstling of his bullock, and his horns are like the horns of unicorns: with them he shall push the people together to the ends of the earth: and they are the ten thousands of Ephraim, and they are the thousands of Manasseh " (Deut. xxxiii. 17).

HIS BIRTH. We consider Ephraim first because of the order of the names upon the Breastplate and because of his priority of position, but in point of fact he was not

103

the firstborn. Manasseh, his brother, was the elder of the two. To have a proper understanding, maybe it will be wise to deal with the two together before considering them individually.

Whilst Joseph was in Egypt he was given a Gentile bride, Asenath, the daughter of Poti-pherah, priest of On, who bore him two sons. The first he named Manasseh meaning " forgetfulness ". " For God," said he, " hath made me forget all my toil and all my father's house." The second son he called Ephraim, meaning " doubly fruitful ", saying at his birth, " For God hath caused me to be fruitful in the land of my affliction." Just before the death of Jacob, Joseph brought these his two sons to his father that he might bless them. Whereupon Jacob sat upon his bed and, wittingly crossing his hands, he placed the right hand upon the younger and the left upon the elder, giving the blessing of the firstborn to the younger. Joseph sought to correct his father but Jacob assured him that his action was deliberate and that the older should serve the younger. From then on we never read of Manasseh and Ephraim, but always Ephraim and Manasseh.

In his act of blessing Jacob also said : " And now thy two sons, Ephraim and Manasseh, which were born unto thee in the land of Egypt before I came unto thee into Egypt, are mine; as Reuben and Simeon, they shall be mine " (Gen. xlviii. 5), and " The Angel which redeemed me from all evil, bless the lads; and let my name be named on them " (Gen. xlviii. 16). In the first reference it is not only to be seen that Jacob adopted these two grandsons of his into his own family but that he gave to them an equality with the firstborn — " As Reuben and Simeon, they shall be mine ". Reuben was the beginning of his strength. How often it is that we find the

Lord crosses our purposes and brings our despised and rejected " Ephraims " to the very front rank of blessing — it may be that troublesome child in our Sunday School from whom we expect nothing but diappointment, it may be the unnoticed, almost despised, person in the Church, it might be some talent or gift in your own life upon which you have put no value. You may have prayed : " Lord, bless me in this thing," and instead you have found Him to bless you in that other thing. Like Joseph, maybe you were disappointed at the time. But oh! How we have to thank Him for His Wisdom, because His Wisdom always proves to be greater than our requests. Thus these two men became two of the tribes of Israel, and were the double portion of Joseph who never found himself to become a tribe in name. It was in this way that they both found a place upon the Breastplate as tribes, although they were never named on the shoulder-stones as sons by birth.

HIS BLESSING. " And the name of the second called he Ephraim : For God hath caused me to be fruitful in the land of my affliction." Joseph little realised all that was pertaining to that name. As already stated it means " doubly fruitful ", and when Jacob set him above his brother and bestowed upon him the blessing of the firstborn he became the inheritor of the double portion of the firstborn. So far as is known Joseph had no other children apart from.these two born to him in Egypt during the seven years of plenty. The increase of Joseph's posterity was, therefore, in these two sons and especially in Ephraim. The Book of Genesis closes by telling us that Joseph saw Ephraim's children of the third generation. When the tribes of Israel were numbered Ephraim stood at 40,500 against Manasseh at 32,000. Moses conveys exactly the same thought to us in his blessing of

Joseph when he said: " His (Joseph's) glory is like the firstling of his bullock, and his horns are like the horns of unicorns: with them he shall push the people together to the ends of the earth: and they are the ten thousands of Ephraim, and they are the thousands of Manasseh," meaning that the strength of the advance of Joseph and the establishment of his family was in his two sons, but particularly in Ephraim.

God had caused Joseph to become fruitful and prosperous in the land of his affliction. How true it often is! " For our light affliction which is but for a moment, worketh for us a far more exceeding and eternal weight of glory " (2 Cor. iv. 17). It did not appear so to Joseph. Follow that hazardous life of his. He might easily have said: " Why did my brothers hate me? It was not my fault that my father favoured me. Why did they misunderstand my dreams? I never told them with any pride or conceit in my heart. When my father sent me to Shechem to my brethren, why did I not return home instead of pursuing them on to Dothan? Why did that caravan of traders come along just at that particular time so that I should be sold to them? Why was Potiphar's wife so cruel and deceitful to me? Why should I receive evil for doing good? Why the prison? Why did the butler forget to plead my cause? Why! Why!! Why!!!?" This is how we often reflect on life. This is how Joseph could have reflected, and possibly did. But take away any one of those experiences and the sequence of events has broken down, and Joseph could never have found his way to the second throne of Egypt, his name would never have been Zaphnath-paaneah, meaning, according to the Vulgate: " The saviour of the age." Yes, indeed, they meant it for evil but God meant it for good.

We must learn that the life submitted to the Lord is overruled by Him so that ALL things work TOGETHER for GOOD to them that love Him. " . . . tribulation worketh patience; and patience, experience; and experience, hope; and hope maketh not ashamed; because the love of God is shed abroad in our hearts by the Holy Ghost which is given unto us " (Rom. v. 3-5). We, who are the " Ephraims " of the Lord, live because our Joseph, the Lord Jesus Christ, came into the Egypt of this world and through the hate and the misunderstanding, the trials and the mockings, found His way via the Cross into the prison of the tomb and death; then the third day, being delivered from His imprisonment because death could not keep Him and corruption could not be His lot, He arose from the grave, ascended on high, and is now seated on the Throne of His eternal glory, and is ministering the Bread of Life to His people as well as presenting their cause before the Father.

There is also another, a prophetic, picture to be seen in this story of Joseph and his two sons and the reversed blessings of Jacob being bestowed upon them. Two great peoples have and do exist in this world, their records are to be found in the annals of God revealing their beginning and their end. They each hold a great prominence in the history of the world. The first is the seed of Abraham according to promise, or Israel. This nation is referred to as the son of God and is the firstborn. This the Lord declared to Pharaoh through Moses when He said : " And I say unto thee, Let my son go, that he may serve Me; and if thou refuse to let him go, behold, I will slay thy son, even thy firstborn " (Exod. iv. 23). This people would be seen in Manasseh. The second great company is the Church of Christ which came into being long after and so would be represented by Ephraim. In

the course of time Israel forgot their God. They crucified their Messiah and thus we see God, as it were, crossing His Hands so that, whilst both peoples are to enjoy
the blessings of the Lord, the double blessing of the firstborn has fallen out to the Church — " the elder shall
serve the younger " as the Lord had said. The Church
is younger than Israel by some 2,000 years, and yet we
are going to reign with Christ and, when we do, Israel
will be the people over whom we shall reign.

THE LIGURE. This is tne stone of the Breastplate
upon which the name of Ephraim was written, but very
little is known concerning it. Commentators differ a
good deal in their suggestions although most of them
would say that it was possibly the modern jacinth or yellow jargoon. Flinders Petrie identifies it with the yellow
agate. The uncertainty of it causes one to refrain from
seeking any spiritual application.

CHAPTER XVI

AGATE — MANASSEH

Gen. xli. 51; xlviii. 16; *Exod.* xxviii. 19; *Deut.* xxxiii. 17

" And Joseph called the name of the firstborn Manasseh: For God, said he, hath made me forget my toil, and all my father's house " (Gen. xli. 51).

" The Angel which redeemed me from all evil, bless the lads; and let my name be named on them, and the name of my fathers Abraham and Isaac; and let them grow into a multitude in the midst of the earth " (Gen. xlviii. 16).

" His glory is like the firstling of his bullock, and his horns are like the horns of unicorns: with them he shall push the people together to the ends of the earth: and they are the ten thousands of Ephraim, and they are the thousands of Manasseh " (Deut. xxxiii. 17).

HIS BIRTH. This chapter must necessarily be read in connection with the previous chapter because the record of the birth of the two sons of Joseph is given as a joint record, and there is no purpose in reiterating what has already been stated. This one thing might be added in favour of Manasseh, who had lost his position as firstborn to the advantage of his younger brother. It is that no reason whatever appears to be given as to why Jacob reversed the blessing. There is no evidence of sin, slackness, nor unworthiness in this character, as is found in the story concerning Jacob and Esau with the transfer of birthright and blessing. It is the second time that such an act had been performed by Jacob, for Joseph, the father of these lads, had received preference in his younger days which had created a hatred amongst his brethren. Now Jacob is doing it again, and although Joseph may protest, his protestation cannot be brought to an issue nor even carry very much weight seeing he had enjoyed these favours even though they may have brought him through some deep waters. The vital point is that, although it was customary to bestow the double portion upon the firstborn, the father had the right to bestow it upon whom he chose. Maybe that Jacob detected something in the character of Ephraim that was more steadfast, or maybe God guided him to bestow it upon the man who in future days would use such powers best. Be assured that the Lord, Who knows our lives and Who knows our end from our beginning, will mete out His blessing according to His Divine Wisdom and Foreknowledge. This means blessing for the receiver, but it does not necessarily mean judgment to the person who has not received that favour.

HIS BLESSING. Joseph's statement: " *And Joseph called the name of his firstborn Manasseh: For God, he said, hath made me forget all my toil, and all my father's house*" — Forgetfulness. There is a forgetfulness which is a vice and should be severely shunned, and there is a forgetfulness which is a virtue and should be wholeheartedly embraced. It is the latter that is considered here. In the natural order of things Joseph named his firstborn " Forgetting ", and his second " Fruitful ". That is the correct order. When we forget the things which are behind, when we forget self and sin, then it is that the Lord makes us to become fruitful and that fruitfulness soon begins to take the first place under His guidance. Paul seeks to emphasise this when he says: " Forgetting those things which are behind, and reaching forth unto those things which are before, I press towards the mark for the prize of the high calling of God in Christ Jesus " (Phil. iii. 13-14).

This statement of Joseph's does not therefore suggest an intolerance or indifference towards his father and his home, subsequent events proved this. " God hath made me forget all my toil." In the joy of the present he could afford to forget the sorrow of the past, the wrong, the injustice, the bitter way he had been made to walk by the actions of his brethren, and later by the conduct of Potiphar's wife and the forgetfulness of the butler. These were the things God had allowed him to forget. Alas, how many Christians live on their past! They nurse in their bosoms all the wrongs that have ever been done to them. They embalm them in an unforgiving spirit so that they may ever have them for display when it suits them, and then they wonder why it is that the Lord never gives them an " Ephraim " of fruitfulness. Have you any cherished grievances? Away with them, put a millstone around them and let them sink to the bottom of the sea, for they are a poison to your spiritual life. Pray God that you may give birth to a Manasseh for until you have brought forth this firstborn there can never be an Ephraim. It was the joy of a son of his own, the building up of his own family, that caused his father's house (the old life) to take a second place. It is the joy that comes through the Son of God finding a place in our lives that changes all relationships. Joseph, like Paul, was now crucified to the old things and alive to the new. Oh, no! He was not neglectful of his brethren, neither had he forgotten parental care. He maintained the full honour of his manhood, he was not looking back to the old home with the unhappy relationships. He was looking forward to meeting his father and his brethren again — not backward, forward.

Jacob's Statement. " The Angel which redeemed me from all evil, bless the lads." The Angel, being spelt with a capital A, was the Lord; no doubt the same Angel which wrestled with Jacob at Penuel until the breaking of the day, the Angel that changed Jacob, the supplanter, into Israel, the Prince, and in so doing redeemed that life from the destruction to which it was doomed. That same Angel which did such great things for me, bless the lads! Guard them, too, from the evils of life, redeem them from the perils of the way. No greater request could be made for these his grandchildren — or, rather, his adopted sons. " . . . let them grow into a multitude in the midst of the earth." These two men grew into two tribes numbering 72,700, second only to Judah, and they stretched across the centre of Palestine which is " in the midst of the earth ". Finally there is

Moses' Statement. " His (Joseph's) glory is like the firstlings of his bullock and his horns are like the horns of unicorns." If you will look at a map of Palestine showing the tribes, you will see that Ephraim and half the tribe of Manasseh stretch from the coast to the River Jordan which runs down the centre of the land. The other half tribe of Manasseh reaches from the other side of the River Jordan to the border of Syria — thus the two tribes between them stretch right across the land like two great horns.

A great deal of history could be recorded concerning these tribes but this must be left. Perhaps two geographical notes would interest readers to show how they fit in with the blessings of Jacob and Moses concerning Joseph.

Manasseh — half of which existed each side of Jordan, hence the continual reference to the half tribe of Manasseh. " This division of this tribe may be accounted for on the supposition that the warlike section preferred to settle on the mountainous region of the north east, whilst the more agricultural section preferred to adhere to the western tribes.

" The Manassites of the east of Jordan are described as the descendants of Machir. Under the leadership of Jair they won the northern part of the Trans-Jordanic territory. They were well fitted to inhabit this difficult country and to defend the passes of the north " (F. Marshall, M.A.).

Ephraim — including half tribe of Manasseh. " It was emphatically a good land, including the plain of Sharon, famous for its fertility. The position was central and though rugged in many parts was broken up into wide plains in the heart of the mountains and diversified both in hill and valley by streams of running water and by continuous tracts of verdure and vegetation " (Stanley).

AGATE. Manasseh's name was inscribed on an agate and set into the Breastplate. The agate is a semi-translucent compound mineral which, when cut and polished, produces beautiful and precious variegated stones. The agate is harder than steel and, being rustless, is often used instead of steel in certain scientific instruments. These stones were originally found at Achates in Sicily from whence the name is derived. When found they are rough and unattractive, when split and polished they are a source of delight. Manasseh although second to Ephraim and deprived of the first blessing yet he became a large tribe, a tribe that was split in two so that half dwelt on each·side of the River Jordan, being made of service both here and there.

CHAPTER XVII

AMETHYST — BENJAMIN

Gen. xxxv. 16-20; xlix. 27; *Exod.* xxviii; *Deut.* xxxiii. 12

" And as they journeyed from Bethel; and there was but a little way to come to Ephrath: and Rachel travailed, and she had hard labour. And it came to pass, when she was in hard labour, that the midwife said unto her: Fear not; thou shalt have this son also. And it came to pass, as her soul was in departing (for she died), that she called his name Benoni: but his father called him Benjamin. And Rachel died, and was buried in the way to Ephrath, which is Bethlehem " (Gen. xxxv. 16-20).

" Benjamin shall ravin as a wolf: in the morning he shall devour the prey and at night he shall divide the spoil " (Gen. xlix. 27).

" And of Benjamin he said, The beloved of the Lord shall dwell in safety by him; and the Lord shall cover him all the day long, and he shall dwell between his shoulders " (Deut. xxxiii. 12).

HIS BIRTH. The story surrounding the birth of Benjamin is a sad one. If one reflects for a moment it will be remembered that Rachel was the favourite wife of Jacob but she was in great distress because God had withholden from her the fruit of the womb, the coveted possession of all Eastern women. She had on several occasions sought to force an issue. It was she who first made the suggestion of giving her handmaid to her husband as a wife, hoping thereby to obtain children by an adoption. On another occasion, in bitterness of soul she said to Jacob: " Give me children, or else I die ". For this her husband had to reprove her saying: " Am I in God's stead, who hath withheld from thee the fruit of the womb . . . " (Gen. xxx. 2). In the course of time God gave her a son and she called his name Joseph, saying: " The Lord shall add to me another son " (Gen. xxx. 24). Here she is seen seeking to force things with God in prophesying a second son. God gave her that second son but it cost her her life. She said: " Give me children, or else I die ". God gave her children and she died in childbirth.

What a picture of the folly of demanding prayer! We need to learn a complete resignation to the Divine Will. Thus it was that this tragedy befell Rachel and Jacob. They were on a journey, and not very far from Bethlehem when a halt was called. Rachel could go no farther and so by the way she laboured. The midwife sought to comfort her by assuring her that this too was a son and that all would be well, but in her anguish she named him Benoni, meaning " The son of my sorrow ". She died and there she was buried by the wayside, and Rachel's tomb can be seen hard by the road to this very day. Jacob was not happy about the name of this son. It was too much of a reminder to him of the sorrow of his beloved Rachel, and so he changed the name from Benoni to Benjamin, " The son of my right hand."

The thought of demanding prayer does not end here. It can be found throughout the whole of the history of Israel. Even in connection with the tribe of Benjamin it occurs again. A time came when the children of Israel demanded a king. They were warned of the consequences but still they pressed their demand. So a king was given who came from the tribe of Benjamin — Saul — and they lived to regret their demand. Let us beware, let us pray: " Thy will be done."

Whilst musing around the names Benoni and Benjamin with their meanings, " Son of sorrow " and " Son of my right hand ", we would remind ourselves that the Son of God's Right Hand, the Lord Jesus Christ, became for us the " Man of Sorrows ". Benjamin was the only son who was named by his father. Jesus too was named by His Father, for God hath " given Him a name which is above every Name that at the Name of Jesus every knee should bow ". The reason why Jacob loved Benjamin above all the others was the fact that he cost him the life of Rachel, the wife who was so dear to him. In that sense we who are Christians are all " Benjamins ", because we cost the Eternal God the life of His only begotten Son to give us eternal life and to make us to become the Sons of God.

One more thought concerning the birth. It is that three great characteristic men were born in Bethlehem — Benjamin, " The son of my right hand " — David, The Beloved, Israel's greatest King — and Jesus, The Son of God, great David's greater Son. A wonderful line of truth can be gathered by connecting these names with each other. (As it is not our present theme, it is just mentioned in passing.)

THE PATRIARCHAL BLESSING. " *Benjamin shall ravin as a wolf* : *in the morning he shall devour the prey and at night he shall divide the spoil.*" At first reading this sounds to be quite foreign to the character of Benjamin as we usually imagine him. This may be due to the fact that, as he was the youngest, he is so often thought of as the boy, and also because of his father's concern for his protection at the time he refused to allow him to accompany his brethren into Egypt. In point of fact Benjamin was a fully matured man. Whatever the quality of character that was in Benjamin as an individual, the above statement is amazingly true of him as a tribe, " Benjamin shall ravin as a wolf." If consideration is given to all that is recorded in the Scriptures concerning this tribe it will be agreed that it was a warring tribe, always on the prowl seeking for prey. The Book of Judges gives a fine example of the exploits of this tribe. Suffice it here to state some of the well-known records.

Ehud, the left-handed warrior, who fought and afterwards judged Israel, was of this tribe (Judges iii. 12-30).

Israel's first king, Saul, the son of Kish, was a Benjamite. Listen to his reply to Samuel: " . . . Am not I a Benjamite, of the smallest of the tribes of Israel? And my family the least of all the families of the tribe of Benjamin . . . ?" (1 Sam. ix. 21.) Saul knew how to ravin like a wolf.

Jonathan would, of course, be of the same tribe.

Mordecai and Esther, who were undoubtedly called of God for a time and a purpose, made a great destruction of the enemies of the Jews, and enjoyed the evening of their lives in the place of power and authority, were of the same tribe (Esther ii. 5).

Of all the characters that could be named the greatest was the one who once said: " For I also am an Israelite, of the seed of Abraham, of the tribe of Benjamin " (Rom. xi. 1). Paul tells the Philippians the same fact. " Circumcised the eighth day, of the stock of Israel, of the tribe of Benjamin . . . " (Phil. iii. 5). Could anything be more characteristic of Paul? In the morning of his life like a wolf he ravaged the Church laying hands on whom he would, haling them into prison. In the evening of his life he shared in the sufferings of the saints. In the morning he ravined and fiercely devoured as a persecutor; in the evening of old age he shared the spoils of a preacher, dividing his experiences and his wisdom to others.

May we in the morning of our lives ravage the bulwarks of Satan, then in the eventide divide our spoil, giving our trophies, our victories, our thanksgiving to the Lord and our experiences to others.

THE MOSAIC BLESSING. " And of Benjamin he said, The beloved of the Lord shall dwell in safety by him; and the Lord shall cover him all the day long, and he shall dwell between his shoulders." The shoulders are the symbol of strength. It is here that the heavy burden is carried. It was there that the shepherd bore his lamb. But the significance is more precise than the general idea of the shoulder of strength. The mother in Palestine rests and carries her child in a cradle made of goats' hair which she is able to sling over her head so that, with a band round her forehead, the baby is resting in its cradle between her shoulders, being suspended from her head. Her large veil, worn as a headdress, is pulled over the cradle to help keep both the sun and the flies off the child. With the child in this safe place where no harm can befall it the mother will walk abroad, shopping, visiting, etc. The thought behind the verse is, therefore, one of devotion. Mother and child are always together, the child is never left behind. So the promise was that the Lord would not leave Benjamin in his need but would always give him the fondness, care, protection, and covering that a mother gave her infant.

What was promised to Benjamin the Lord has promised to those of us who are His children. " I will never leave thee nor forsake thee."

THE AMETHYST. To quote from a Bible Diction-ary: " It is agreed that the common amethyst, properly called amethystine quartz, is meant. This is rock crystal coloured purple by manganese and iron. The Oriental amethyst is a much rarer gem, composed of violet corundum (oxide of aluminium) — in short, a purple sapphire. The name of the amethyst is derived from its supposed property, no doubt associated with its wine-like colour, of acting as a preventive of intoxication."

The English Dictionary says: " A bluish-violet kind of quartz, formerly supposed to prevent intoxication (Gk. a-methustos, not drunken; from methuein, be drunk)." It was a stone of great hardness. How this might apply to Benjamin as an individual might be difficult to say, if it applied at all; but some relationship might be found in the tribe. They were hard and oft-times headstrong in their warlike character. At one time this tribe of 26,700 faced 40,000 in battle after wronging a Levite in abusing and killing his wife. It is a gruesome story in Judges xix and xx, perhaps summed up in the word intoxication. When Saul, the Benjamite, persecuted the Christians, he was " exceedingly mad " against them and stopped at nothing, travelling far and taking women and children. He was intoxicated with anger. They needed therefore the influence and the power of God to bring them into discipline and self control. Was that the rea-son why God placed this name indelibly on an Amethyst?

CHAPTER XVIII

BERYL — DAN

Gen. xxx. 1-6; *Gen.* xlix. 16-18; *Exod.* xxviii. 20;
Deut. xxxiii. 22

" And when Rachel saw that she bare Jacob no children, Rachel envied her sister; and said unto Jacob, Give me children or else I die. And Jacob's anger was kindled against Rachel: And he said, Am I in God's stead, who hath withheld from thee the fruit of the womb? And she said, Behold my maid Bilhah, go in unto her; and she shall bear upon my knees, that I may also have children by her. And she gave him Bilhah her handmaid to wife: and Jacob went in unto her. And Bilhah conceived, and bare Jacob a son. And Rachel said, God hath judged me, and hath also heard my voice, and hath given me a son: therefore called she his name Dan " (Gen. xxx. 1-6).

" Dan shall judge his people, as one of the tribes of Israel. Dan shall be a serpent by the way, an adder in the path, that biteth the horse heels; so that his rider shall fall backward. I have waited for thy salvation, O Lord " (Gen. xlix. 16-18).

" And of Dan he said, Dan is a lion's whelp, he shall leap from Bashan " (Deut. xxx. 22).

HIS BIRTH. The character of Rachel was one of impatience and jealousy. As a result of her barrenness she had taken a despairing view of life, so that she approached her husband in a vindictive manner, saying:

"Give me children, or else I die," by which she meant "Deliver me from my barrenness or I am as a dead woman despised and unwanted". She thereby kindled the anger of her husband and so became responsible for a general disturbance in the relationship of the whole family. In her determination she adopted unlawful expedients by giving her handmaid to her husband, hoping that she might get some claim upon a child and become a mother by proxy. This revealed a lack of trust in God. Her plan succeeded for the moment and as she took this child of Bilhah, she said: "God hath judged me," and she called his name Dan, which means "Judge". It is suggested that the statement "God hath judged me" would be more correctly expressed "hath procured for me justice," thus conveying the idea that the Lord had supported her in her unlawful effort and had vindicated her from her humiliation, but we are yet to learn that the tribe of Dan was responsible for humiliating all Israel on more than one occasion through its idolatry.

THE PATRIARCHAL BLESSING. "*Dan shall judge his people as one of the tribes.*" Notice it does not say that Dan shall judge the tribes, even though he may have ascended to that position at one time when Samson, a member of that tribe, governed Israel during the period of the Judges. What Jacob said was: "Dan shall judge his people *as one of* the tribes." Not as a superior but as an equal, not judging others but judging himself, and if he did judge others it was on the ground of mutuality. This one feels is an important point, because it holds a great lesson for us. We have had judgment given unto us, for we are to judge ourselves as believers. Listen to the exhortation of the Apostle Paul: "But let a man examine himself, and so let him eat of that bread, and drink of that cup " (1 Cor. xi. 28). Again: " For if we would judge ourselves, we should not be judged " (1 Cor. xi. 31). None of us likes to be judged by others. The solution to that dislike is to keep our own lives under a self judgment according to the standards of God's Word. This, of course, is a personal matter. Then there is the judgment of one's own community. " Dan shall judge his people." Paul applies this to the Church in its own several communities. " For what have I to do to judge them also that are wtihout? *Do not ye judge them that are within*? But them that are without God judgeth " (1 Cor. v. 12-13).

" *Dan shall be a serpent by the way, an adder in the path, that biteth the horse heels, so that his rider shall fall backward.*" This creature, to which Dan was likened, was the horneu serpent of the colour of sand and marked with white and black spots, which was exceedingly dangerous to passers by. Merely stretching out its feelers it inflicted a fatal wound. In this connection there are two outstanding pictures in which Dan takes the leading role.

The first picture is that of Israel's idolatry. The nation was warned of God's hatred of idolatry and of the consequences of engaging in such misconduct. Israel fell to this vice and lost her prestige and, consequently, like the horse rider, was brought down to the ground. Dan was the tribe responsible for this fatal nip. True it began in one man in the tribe, but presently the whole tribe was affected and then the nation. The first little subtle " bite " was when the children of Dan found an image in the house of Micah, as recorded in Judges xviii. They took it from the man and made it their own as a people. " And the children of Dan set up the graven image: and Jonathan, the son of Gershom, the son of Manasseh, he and his sons were priests to the tribe of Dan until the day of the captivity of the land. And they set them up Micah's graven image, which he made, all the time that the house of God was in Shiloh " (Judges xviii. 30-31). Later on, in the reign of Jeroboam, he sets up two golden calves. " And he set the one in Bethel, and the other put he in Dan. And this thing became a sin : for the people went to worship before the one, even unto Dan " (1 Kings xii. 29-30). Thus the sin of one man extended to the tribe and from the tribe to the nation, and so the nation was brought down, surely by " a serpent by the way ". Let us watch carefully our smallest short-comings, our secret sins. They may affect a whole community.

The other picture referred to is the scene of Judges xvi. There was Samson, a member of the tribe of Dan, and a Judge in Israel. Watch his deterioration as he gave away to his enemy the secret of his great strength, until the enemy he once mastered had become his master. In utter shame, weak, blind and helpless, he was led by a lad into the great auditorium where the Philistines sought to make sport of him. Three thousand were away on the roof and great was their glee, but Samson, the Danite, prayed that the Lord God would remember him and give him back his strength this once that he might " bite " at the heels of these his enemies and bring them down in the midst of their pride. God answered his prayer and he, bowing himself upon those support-ing pillars, brought the whole building and the Phili-stines down to their death. God make us " as wise as serpents and as harmless as doves " that, in our faith-fulness to the Lord, we may be used to break down the strongholds of Satan, and bring the enemies of the Cross down to their knees in repentance and in an acknowledgment of Christ Jesus as Lord.

"*I have waited for thy salvation, O Lord.*"   This eighteenth verse seems to have nothing to do with the blessing of Dan nor of any other of the tribes. The verse almost appears out of place or as though, in the midst of blessing his sons, Jacob is suddenly carried away in the Spirit beyond the fortunes of these tribes with all their battles and their victories, beyond all the things national, to the triumphant, permanent victory of the Messiah. "I have waited for *thy* salvation, O Lord." The thought may be verified by the Jewish Targums in which this translation is found: "Our father, Jacob, said, Not for the salvation of Gideon, the son of Joash, does my soul look out, for that is only temporary, and not for the salvation of Samson, for that is only transient, but for the salvation promised in Thy Word for Thy people, the sons of Israel; for that salvation does my soul look out."

THE MOSAIC BLESSING. " And he said of Dan, Dan is a lion's whelp : he shall leap from Bashan." Not that Dan, shall leap from Bashan, but that he should leap out suddenly as the lions of Bashan were known to leap out from the forests upon the unwary traveller.   All commentators are agreed that this has a possible reference to an incident recorded in Joshua xix. 47, when the children of Dan displayed another kind of judgment, one of severity, when, considering that their territory was too small, they suddenly pounced upon a neighbouring people dwelling quietly and securely and took possession of their land and named it after their father, Dan. The lion of the tribe of Dan differed considerably from the Lion of the tribe of Judah. The Lord make us followers of the latter.

THE BERYL. This stone, on which Dan's name was registered on the Breastplate, is a very hard stone. The name Beryl means " to break or subdue ". It is referred to in Ezekiel in connection with the swift and powerful chariots and wheels seen by the prophet (Ezek. x. 9). The hands of the Bridegroom, in the Song of Solomon, are set with beryl (S. of S. v. 14). Sufficient has been learned to see why this stone was chosen for Dan, the judge who was ever breaking or subduing in one form or another. The Lord make us hard Beryls " breaking and subduing " wherever we meet the forces of sin and the strength of Satan, and that, of course, in His strength not ours.

CHAPTER XIX

ONYX — ASHER

Gen. xxx. 12-13; *Gen.* xlix. 20; *Exod.* xxviii. 20; *Deut.* xxxiii. 24-25

"And Zilpah, Leah's maid, bare Jacob a second son. And Leah said, Happy am I, for the daughters will call me blessed: and she called his name Asher" (Gen. xxx. 12-13).

"Out of Asher his bread shall be fat, and he shall yield royal dainties" (Gen. xlix. 20).

"And of Asher he said, Let Asher be blessed with children; let him be acceptable to his brethren, and let him dip his foot in oil. Thy shoes shall be iron and brass; and as thy days, so shall thy strength be" (Deut. xxxiii. 24-25).

HIS BIRTH. This child was the second born of Zilpah and adopted by Leah who was also responsible for naming him. As she took this child into her arms with an air of contentment and pleasure she said: "Happy am I, for the daughters will call me blessed", and she gave him a name which embraced both of the words she used, for Asher means "Happy" or "Blessed". Furthermore, we are given to understand that the Hebrew form of this name is "Ashere", which is plural and often occurs as such in the Hebrew Scriptures. The whole sense of Leah's remark is plural also. Note it — " Happy am *I* for the daughters will call *ME* blessed; and she called *HIM* ' Happy or Blessed '." What was hers became his. This mutuality of blessing is a principle of Christian doctrine. In the Old Testament: "*I will* bless thee and *thou shalt* be a blessing " (Gen. xii. 2). In the New Testament: ". . . that *My joy* might remain in you, and that *your joy* might be full " (John xv. 11). We are blessed of the Lord and yet we are called upon to bless the Lord. This is to be seen again in the Mosaic blessing.

Returning to the Scriptural use of the plural word " Ashere ", this word is twenty-seven times translated in our version as " Blessed " and should always be understood as " Blessednesses " and eighteen times the same word is translated " Happy " and should read: " Happy, very happy." Out of these forty-three references, twenty-seven occur in the Psalms. Here are two well-known verses as examples. " Blessed is the man that walketh not in the counsel of the ungodly " (Ps. i. 1). " Blessed is the man whose sin is covered " (Ps. xxxii. 1). In both the word is " Ashere " in the Hebrew and so should read: " The Blessednesses of the man ". How forceful this is! The man who walks in the path of righteousness with a knowledge that his sin is covered is more than blessed. He is crowned with blessing upon blessing and joy upon joy until, in the ecstasy of the Lord's goodness, he calls upon all that is within him to bless and to praise His Holy Name. In the case of Asher it was not limited to spiritual blessings but his was a prosperous tribe in material fruitfulness. The Lord grant us this fulness.

THE PATRIARCHAL BLESSING. " Out of Asher

his bread shall be fat and he shall yield royal dainties."
With reference to this statement some have sought to
point out the richness of the soil in his allotted territory,
but there is something much deeper than that.   The
whole of the statements concerning Asher reveals quality.
" His bread shall be fat." Christ is the Bread of Life to
His people, and that Bread is not chaffy nor cheap. It is
fat, of high quality, and so satisfies the hungry soul.
Says David : " My soul shall be satisfied with marrow and
fatness ", and again : " They shall be abundantly satisfied with the fatness of Thy house." The corn of Canaan
is far better than the leeks and onions of Egypt. Asher
represents those people who feed upon the " finest of the
wheat ". They know a living, abiding communion with
Christ Himself. The Word of God is their daily portion,
like Job who said : " I have esteemed the words of His
mouth more than my necessary food " (Job xxiii. 12).
The natural result of a healthy intake is a virile output.
    Asher yielded royal dainties — dainties tempting,
attractive, appetising, but wholesome. Because a patient
has lost normal appetite by reason of a run-down condition physically, he is not fed with husks, with water
less the beef extract, with the packet instead of the con-
tents, with the peeling instead of the pear. No! No!!
The wholesome food is necessary, and even more so. Because the vitality of the Church is low just now and
Christians cannot stand the solid meat, the fat bread of
God's Word, many a Church has resorted to the husks
and peelings of sociality and compromise in which the
food value is entirely missing. This is a tragic mistake
and will never make for healthy recovery. Our methods
may have to change, but our material of fundamental
gospel truth must never be substituted.   Men of God
ought so to feed on the fatness of God's Word that, like

Asher, they may give to the people " royal dainties "
straight from the King's banqueting chamber. " A word
fitly spoken is like apples of gold in pictures of silver "
(Prov. xxv. 11).

*THE MOSAIC BLESSING. " And of Asher he said,
Let Asher be blessed with (in his) children."* There are
many interpretations given to this statement of Moses —
" Blessed with many children ", " Blessed above the
sons ", " Blessed of his sons " — all of which ably fit
the character, but as there is a preposition which is always used as denoting the source from which anything
proceeds or the agent by whom anything is done, the interpretation of " Blessed with children " might readily
be accepted as meaning he was to be blessed through his
children who were to reap their benefits from him. This
is a beautiful thought. Asher, in the richness of his own
experience, was to become such an avenue and agent of
blessing that in coming generations his children would
rise up and call him blessed. That is richness of character
indeed, when our influence is so felt by our children and
it has brought such blessing to their lives that they have
to thank God for every remembrance of us. How can
we come into such a richness of blessing? The answer
is simple. If we want to bless the lives of our children
that they may bless us, then let us remember that we
are the children of God and that He is our great Ashere.
He has blessed us abundantly, therefore we must do only
that which will cause men who see our good works to
glorify our Father Who is in Heaven. To the extent that
we bring blessing to His Name, to that same measure
shall we be made a blessing to others.

" Let him be acceptable to his brethren." Oft-times
success, whether in material possessions or in spiritual
qualities and service, brings a jealousy in the hearts of

one's brethren which, as in the case of Joseph's brethren, grows into a hatred that insists on vengeance. Asher was to be delivered from this curse and was to be acceptable amongst them, surely blessedness indeed that ought to make him " happy, very happy ".

"*Let him dip his foot in oil.*" Many have made reference to the fruitfulness of the tribe of Asher as a land of olive groves, and of the pressing out of the olive berries into oil. A modern view is that it might be a prophetic utterance referring to the pipe-line of the Iraq Petroleum Company which passes through Asher and pours out some million gallons of oil daily at Haifa which is also within the boundaries of Asher. These suggestions are very acceptable, but one still feels that the spiritual meaning of these statements is of paramount importance. The richness of the land is no doubt here, but what of the richness of the believer's walk! A foot literally dipped in oil would leave behind it an indelible impression. Says Isaiah : " How beautiful upon the mountains are the feet of him that bringeth good tidings, that publisheth peace; that bringeth good tidings of good, that publisheth salvation; that saith unto Zion, Thy God reigneth!" (Isa. lii. 7). It is not only what we may say now but, like Asher, it is what we leave behind. Succeeding generations rejoiced in the sustained blessings of Asher. May we so dip our feet into the oil of God's Holy Spirit that we may leave behind us that certain imprint which will cause men to say : " These have been with Jesus and learned of Him." There are hundreds like Frances Ridley Havergal, John Wesley, George Muller, William Carey, who have left a holy imprint in hymns, sermons, Homes and Mission fields, for men of all time.

" *Thy shoes shall be iron and brass.*" The word translated "shoes" is elsewhere translated "bolts" or "bars". The whole suggestion is a strong fortification, a trampling underfoot of evil. "Thou shalt tread upon the lion and adder: the young lion and the dragon shalt thou trample under feet" (Ps. xci. 13), or a barricading against the advancing hosts. The fruitful life is the overcoming life. And finally

"*As thy days, so shall thy strength be.*" Many of these words are in italic signifying that they are not in the original text. Leaving these words out so as to see it in its literal rendering, it is: "As thy days thy strength". A strength which will last as long as thy days, or a strength which, like thy days, is ever increasing. There is no suggestion of a fluctuating strength which varies according to circumstances as so many interpret it. It is not according to needs but according to days, and they never fail as long as we are in time.

THE ONYX. It is very difficult to ascertain exactly what stone is referred to as the onyx in the Bible because it is spoken of as being precious and brilliant, and the onyx as it is known to-day is neither. According to Robertson the Hebrew word "Shoh-ham" is derived from an unused root signifying "to shine with the lustre of fire" and "a flashing forth of splendour". If this is so, then it is most characteristic of the tribe whose name it bore. Sufficient has been said in this chapter to show that Asher's character flashed forth with splendour, its glory having reached down even unto us.

CHAPTER XX

JASPER — NAPHTALI

Gen. xxx. 7-8; *Gen.* xlix. 21; *Exod.* xxviii. 20;
Deut. xxxiii. 23

" And Bilhah, Rachel's maid, conceived again, and bare Jacob
a second son. And Rachel said, With great wrestlings have I
wrestled with my sister, and I have prevailed: and she called his
name Naphtali " (Gen. xxx. 7-8).

" Naphtali is a hind let loose: he giveth goodly words " (Gen.
xlix. 21).

" And of Naphtali he said, O Naphtali, satisfied with favour, and
full with the blessing of the Lord: possess thou the west and the
south " (Deut. xxx. 23).

The three sections into which each of the chapters have been
divided, viz. His Birth, The Patriarchal Blessing, and The Mosaic
Blessing, might readily be sub-headed in this chapter, as Wrestling,
Liberty, and Resting, for these three words sum up this character
possibly better than any others.

HIS BIRTH — Wrestling. Like Dan he was born of
Bilhah and adopted by Rachel who felt that her
strugglings to maintain the favour of her husband against
the rivalry of her sister had not altogether been in vain.
Thus she said: " With great wrestlings have I wrestled

133

with my sister, and I have prevailed ". Hence she called
the child Naphtali, meaning " My wrestlings ". One
feels doubtful as to whether they can accept this issue as
a prevailing through wrestling. Some commentators suggest that this reference is to a prevailing in prayer that
would be expressed as a wrestling with God rather than
a wrestling with her sister. We are bidden to " Watch
and Pray ", we are expected to Pray and Work, but one
cannot find any authority for Praying and Plotting — or
dishonest scheming which displays a lack of faith in God
or else a lack of patience with God. To suggest that
Rachel prevailed with God is to suggest that God submitted His approval to bigamy, which He never did.

It is not suggested that Rachel did not pray, nor even
that she did not wrestle in prayer because she did, and
also God heard her prayer and gave her Joseph in re-
sponse to those prayers, but Naphtali was not the result
of a wrestling in prayer. Rachel was successful in her
scheme but success does not always mean that God is in
it, even though Rachel may think so and even though we
allow ourselves to be beguiled. God sometimes permits
us to have our way and yet He need not be in it. God
is always in " faithfulness ", but not necessarily in
" success ". We have some outstanding proofs of this
in Scripture. There was one in the earlier history of this
family and there was another in the life of Rachel her-
self. The first is to be found in the experience of Sarah
when she thought that God would not be able to redeem
His promise concerning a son without her help, so that
she gave her handmaid to Abram resulting in the birth
of Ishmael, but God said : " You have got your Ishmael, I
will bless him, but I am still going to have My way, and
Isaac will come as I have promised " — and he did. It
appeared as though Sarah was successful, but she was

not. Ishmael always proved a " thorn in the flesh ". And now again God would say to Rachel: " You have prevailed in your schemes, but Joseph is to come in My time and in My way."

Rachel perpetuated her wrestlings in naming this child, but Rachel was not alone in her wrestlings; her husband later came to the place where he learned something about wrestling, for God met him on his return journey from Haran and there Jacob was engaged in a wrestling throughout one lonely night which lasted until the break of day. Thus at Penuel did he learn that God must break Jacob before He could make an Israel.

From the beginning of time man has known something of the power of wrestling, sometimes prevailing, sometimes losing in the struggle. How numerous are those strugglings at times. Man wrestles with his conscience, with his habits, with temptation. Children in the tenderness of their years have at times to wrestle with their temper or with other things, little to us but everything to them. Again, nature is ever wrestling. The oak is made strong as it struggles against wind and storm. Man is seen wrestling with nature as he seeks to steer his vessel through the raging gale and the tempestuous seas. Yes! Always wrestling, and it always means that one person or element is defeated and the other is strengthened as it gains the victory.

Think of the wrestlings of Christ! Sin has separated God and man, Satan was laying claim to the human race, and they in their need were crying out for deliverance. In creation God spoke the Word and it was done. By His Word worlds were made and flung into immeasurable space. At His Word the storm is released or witheld, but more than His Mighty Word was needed for spiritual accomplishments. Our new birth is by reason of the travailing of the Son of His love. Wrestling in prayer in Gethsemane, wrestling with Satan on Calvary, wrestling with death within the tomb, Jesus prevailed with God, He defeated Satan, He destroyed death, and thus wrought for us our salvation. Having prevailed in this wrestling, the third day He arose and came forth as " the hind of the morning " which is the quotation of Jacob in his blessing of Naphtali; but before turning to that blessing there is a further thought.

The result of Christ's wrestlings means the birth of many spiritual Naphtalis — believers — and we too must know something of wrestling in our spiritual life for we are called to warfare. Paul speaks of those for whom he travailed until Christ was formed in them (Gal. iv. 19). Again, he says: " For we wrestle not against flesh and blood, but against principalities, against powers, against the rulers of darkness of this world, against spiritual wickedness in high places " (Eph. vi. 12). It is the wrestling that makes strong, healthy, virile Christians.

THE PATRIARCHAL BLESSING — Liberty. " Naphtali is a hind let loose: he giveth goodly words." The hind, or the roe, or the gazelle, is a creature that is graceful, gentle and agile. With a sure foot it bounds to the highest height of the rocky crag beyond the reach of its enemies: the emblem of glorious freedom. The hind has been spoken of as the symbol of a warrior, and in this sense was fitting of Naphtali, the tribe, that was swift and sure in its accomplishments on the battlefield. Here is a picture of a hind caught in a trap or entanglement and having been liberated (by itself or someone else) bounds away upwards to a place of safety.

References in the Bible will give some idea of the nature of this animal. Jacob said: " Naphtali is a hind let loose " — liberty. David said " He maketh my feet

like hind's feet and setteth me upon my high places "
(Ps. xviii. 33) — sureness. Habakkuk says the same in
his last verse. The Bride said: " My beloved is like a
roe or a young hart: behold, he standeth behind our
wall, he looketh forth at the windows, shewing himself
through the lattice " (S. of S. ii. 9) — gentleness. Solomon said: " Let her be as the loving hind " (Prov. v.
19) — loving. Here are some lovely thoughts from the
pen of Henry W. Soltau: " ' Naphtali is a hind let loose:
he giveth goodly words '. May there not be an allusion
to this in that wondrous Psalm of the Cross, the twenty-
second, which is headed, ' To the chief musician upon
Aijeleth Shahar, or to the hind of the morning '. It is
a Psalm in which the deep wrestlings of the soul of
Christ are expressed, the pains of the travail of His soul.
But suddenly it changes from the deep tones of woe to
the joyful song of deliverance. In the midst of the twenty-
first verse resurrection deliverance comes in: ' Thou hast
heard me from the horns of the unicorns '.

" The morning without clouds breaks; the hind is let
loose, and bounds away to the highest places, giving
goodly words, or words of fairness and pleasantness. ' I
will declare Thy name unto my brethren; in the midst
of the Church will I sing praise unto Thee.'

" The hind is also used in the Scripture as an emblem
of gentleness and love. Thus, in the Song of Solomon:
' I charge you, O ye daughters of Jerusalem, by the roes,
and by the hinds of the field, that ye stir not up, nor
awake my love, until he (she) please ' (ii. 7 and iii. 5).
The allusion here is to the gentleness of the hind, which
is easily scared. Again, Prov. v. 19: ' Let her be unto
thee as the loving hind.' Here the hind is used as a symbol of affection.

" The feet of the hind enable it to stand securely upon

the summit of lofty crags, out of the reach of danger, and lifted above the snares and pitfalls of the world below. 'He maketh my feet like hind's feet, and setteth me upon my high places' (2 Sam. xxii. 34. Ps. xviii. 33). 'The Lord God is my strength; and he will make my feet like hind's feet, and he will make me walk upon mine high places' (Hab. iii. 19).

"He that is the Lion of the tribe of Judah is also like the gentle loving hind of Naphtali. On the morning of His resurrection, when God had loosed the pains of death, and He, the Lord of life and glory was bounding up to the highest heavens, still, as the gentle loving hind, He stayed on His path to comfort the heart of Mary and to give her that blessed message to His brethren. 'I am ascending to My Father, and your Father; and to My God, and your God.' The goodly words were given by this Hind of the morning. And He has made our feet like hind's feet; we are raised up together with Him; and we have to stand upon the high places, to which we as believers have thus been exalted; and not to let Satan cast us down from our excellency. We have, as of Naphtali, to wrestle, not against flesh and blood, but against principalities, against powers, against the rulers of the darkness of this world, against spirits or wickedness in the heavenly (or high) places (Eph. vi. 12). But Jehovah God is our strength, His great Priest has known the power of the enemy, and has conquered; and He will enable us to overcome and maintain our stand on high. He will uphold us in our wrestlings against the foe by bringing to our remembrance His throes of anguish on the tree, and by clothing us with His strength."

THE MOSAIC BLESSING — Resting. " *O Naphtali, satisfied with favour, and full with the blessing of the Lord*: *possess thou the west and the south.*" The man who can (like the hind) climb the heights of spiritual attainment, rising above all the carnality of the lower regions, and breathe the fresh air of God's grace and can stand fast in the liberty with which Christ has made him free, is surely the man who is " satisfied with favour and full with the blessing of the Lord ". Moses' blessing appears therefore to be resultant upon Jacob's blessing. This privileged person is now told to possess the west and the south. The man who is full and well-favoured is the man who finds rest to his soul. Naphtali was to possess westward which meant seaward towards the Mediterranean, commerce and communication — and southward which meant sunshine, the realm of beauty and fruitfulness. Naphtali was certainly favoured and full here because his southward border was the northern seashore of Galilee and included Capernaum, Bethsaida, Chorazin, and other places where the Lord ministered mostly in teaching and healing. Is it not worth the dark wrestlings to enter into the joy of these abundant blessings?

> " Jesus, I am resting, resting
> In the joy of what Thou art;
> I am finding out the greatness
> Of Thy loving heart."

THE JASPER. This was the stone of the Breastplate chosen for the name of Naphtali. It can be found in many colours, the commonest being yellow, whilst others are scarlet, red, crimson, green, various browns, and one is green with red spots known as the bloodstone. Some are transparent and others opaque. It is not known what colour the one on the Breastplate was, but it may be fairly certain that it was transparent. In the Book of the Revelation, the One Who sat on the throne in chapter four was like a jasper and a sardine stone. The walls of the Holy City in chapter xxi were of jasper and one of the foundations was of the same. One usually thinks of these as a beautiful yellow, full of lustre, so significant of glory, because when John was describing that heavenly Jerusalem he said he saw it " descending out of heaven from God, having the glory of God, and her light was like unto a stone most precious, even like a jasper stone, clear as crystal ". Do you not think that the character of Naphtali could be summed up like that? A man who, living in the higher realms of a spiritual atmosphere, had a testimony which was as clear as crystal and therefore showed forth the glory of God.

CHAPTER XXI

APPENDIX TO THE STONES

(1) LEVI — JOINING
Gen. xxix. 34; *Gen.* xlix. 5-7; *Deut.* xxxiii. 8-11

" And she conceived again, and bare a son; and said, Now this time will my husband be joined unto me, because I have borne him three sons: therefore was his name called Levi " (Gen. xxix. 34).

" Simeon and Levi are brethren; instruments of cruelty are in their habitations. O my soul, come not thou into their secret; unto their assembly, mine honour, be not thou united: for in their anger they slew a man, and in their selfwill they digged down a wall. Cursed be their anger, for it was fierce; and their wrath, for it was cruel: I will divide them in Jacob, and scatter them in Israel " (Gen. xlix. 5-7).

" And of Levi he said Let thy Thummim and thy Urim be with thy holy one, whom thou didst prove at Massah, and with whom thou didst strive at the waters of Meribah; Who said unto his father and to his mother, I have not seen him; neither did he acknowledge his brethren, nor knew his own children: for they have observed thy word, and kept thy covenant. They shall teach Jacob thy judgments, and Israel, thy law: they shall put incense before thee, and whole burnt sacrifice upon thine altar. Bless, Lord, his substance and accept the work of his hands: smite through the loins of them that rise against him, and of them that hate him that they rise not again " (Deut. xxxiii. 8-11).

THERE are two names of the sons of Jacob which have not come under consideration because their names do not appear on the Stones of the Breastplate. The one is Levi, the separated tribe for holy things; the other is Joseph who, having received a double blessing, found himself represented in the names of his two sons, Ephraim and Manasseh. So to complete the Patriarchal and Mosaic blessings we will include these two characters in our treatise.

HIS BIRTH. Leah's confidence took a big step forward when her third son arrived. When the first two

were born she had hoped to gain a little more of her
husband's love and attention. At the birth of the first she
said: " Surely the Lord hath looked upon my affliction
now therefore will my husband love me ", while at the
arrival of the second her remark was: " Because the
Lord hath heard that I was hated, He hath given me
this son also." Now she is more bold and declares:
" Now this time will my husband be joined unto me."
Thus it was that she called his name Levi, which means
" Joined closely ". There is no evidence in Scripture that
this passionate longing of hers was ever realised. If one
may stay to add a further remark in connection with the
two previous names it will be remembered, when considering Reuben and Simeon, we thought of their names
in connection with Christ and the Church, and it was
noted that we were in Jesus, to " See a Son ", and then to
"Hear" Him. "Seeing Him as the Son of God and "hearing" Him as the same means that we shall be "joined" to
Him in a new life. The connection is certainly interesting and suggestive. The fourth son, Judah, gives the
result of the three acts, for his name means the " Praise
of Jehovah "

To return to Levi at the time of his birth, the meaning of his name was apparently not realised by Leah.
Therefore it might be said that being a failure there is
no purpose in considering it, as it cannot convey its in-
tended lesson. May we make bold to say that, whilst Leah
thought she was responsible for the naming and that
she had a strategy which would force an issue with her
husband, actually God was controlling the naming that
thereby He might disclose His purposes.

All these names become a play upon words. In this
character we will dwell on the two words "joined " and
" scattered " which are an antithesis.

THE PATRIARCHAL BLESSING. It was Leah, Levi's mother, who said " joined ", but Jacob, his father, said " scattered " — " I will divide them in Jacob and scatter them in Israel." It was observed in the chapter on Simeon why Levi was scattered. It was because of a gross sin and sin always has a devastating effect.

The tribe, having no inheritance, was given several cities by each of the other tribes, forty-eight cities in all, but these cities were scattered all over the land (Num. xxxv). Therefore Levi was found in little communities throughout Israel. Here is seen a wonderful picture of the Grace of God operating in the Old Testament. Says Paul: " Where sin abounded grace did much more abound ". Sin had separated all mankind from God, yet God desired that those thus separated might be re-united to Himself. Therefore He made a temporary provision by means of offerings and sacrifices but some-one must minister these on the behalf of man. So it was that God chose the scattered tribe of Levi for this priestly work of joining men to God through sacrifice. Thus the man who fell deeply into sin was the man who in his descendants was lifted high in holiness. Was it because " he that is forgiven much loveth much?" At any rate Levi became closely joined to God in service and closely joined to all the other tribes in Tabernacle ministry.

The thought is that there must be a scattering before there can be a gathering, there must be a dividing before there can be a joining. The suggestion is certainly conveyed through the New Testament. Said Jesus: " . . . . I came not to send peace, but a sword. For I am come to set a man at variance against his father . . . " (Matt. x. 34-35). Again, " Everyone that hath forsaken houses, or brethren, or sisters, or father, or mother, or wife, or children, or lands, for My Name's sake, shall receive an hundredfold, and shall inherit everlasting life. But many that are first shall be last; and the last shall be first " (Matt. xix. 29-30). The person who desires to be joined to Christ in happy fellowship must be separated from the world, its sins, and its fashions.

THE MOSAIC BLESSING. The blessing of Moses upon Levi appears to be a revoking of the judgment given by Jacob. As Moses was himself a member of this tribe he has to be careful in giving a reason why it was possible to do this. Moses sought for this tribe a continuance of the priestly privilege (Thummim and Urim) because they had proved themselves worthy at Massah and Meribah. There were two experiences of testing at the waters, one at the beginning of their wilderness journeyings and the other towards the end. The first is recorded in Exod. xvii. 1-7, and the second in Num. xx. 1-13). Both were murmurings of the people against their leaders because of lack of water. As the first and last they may well represent the whole of Israel's murmurings against Moses and Aaron, the representatives of Levi, but throughout these two men proved faithful, except during the sad lapse of Aaron's in the matter of the Golden Calf and for a nasty slip in the last incident, a failing which cost Moses his entrance into the Promised Land.

In none of these bitter trials did these leaders of the tribe of Levi lift up the sword of revenge. Yet there was one time when they had to take up the sword. On that occasion it was not for personal revenge but at the command of God. The people had committed a great sin against their God in the setting up and worshipping of the golden calf (Exod. xxxii). Moses called for those who were on the Lord's side to step out, and all the sons of Levi came forward. Moses said to these men, in effect,

" Here is an opportunity of consecrating yourselves against the treacherous act which has brought so much shame on your tribe. Let every man put his sword to his side. Now go out and use it again, but you must slay your brother, your neighbour, your companion, whoever has sinned against God. Slay him, spare not, take no pity on those who are your kinsmen." What they sowed, they reaped. This is the possible meaning of the next clause of the Mosaic blessing: " Who said unto his father and to his mother I have not seen him; neither did he acknowledge his brethren, nor knew his own children."

Thus their position was reversed and those that were divided in *Jacob* and scattered in *Israel* had it said of them, " They shall teach *Jacob* thy judgments, and *Israel* thy law." Saul, the persecutor of the early Church, having been met by the Lord became Paul, the teacher of the early Church. The sinner, who hated Jesus, through conversion becomes the saint who loves Jesus because He is his Saviour. Thus the " scattered " become the " joined ".

One final word — said Moses: " Bless, Lord, his substance, and accept the work of his hands." He had no territory to bless, no fields to multiply, no coasts to protect, so the blessing was upon his substance, his personal possessions, and upon the service he rendered to the nation as a whole. His enemies were not national nor tribal for he had no territory to lose, so they had none to gain. His enemies would more likely be spiritual. Moses asked for a complete and final deliverance from such.

Learn that Jesus can take a sinner and make him a saint. He can take the beggar from the dunghill and set him upon the throne of His glory and then give him the victory over all things.

(2) JOSEPH — FRUITFUL

Gen. xxx. 22-24; *Gen.* xlix. 22-26; *Deut.* xxxiii. 13-17

" And God remembered Rachel, and God hearkened to her, and opened her womb. And she conceived and bare a son; and said, God hath taken away my reproach: And she called his name Joseph: and said, The Lord shall add to me another son " (Gen. xxx. 22-24).

" Joseph is a fruitful bough, even a fruitful bough by a well; whose branches run over the wall: The archers have sorely grieved him, and shot at him, and hated him: but his bow abode in strength, and the arms of his hands were made strong by the hands of the mighty God of Jacob; (from thence is the shepherd the stone of Israel): Even by the God of thy father, who shall help thee; and by the Almighty, who shall bless thee with blessings of heaven above, blessings of the deep that lieth under, blessings of the breasts, and of the womb: The blessings of thy father have prevailed above the blessings of my progenitors unto the utmost bound of the everlasting hills: they shall be on the head of Joseph, and on the crown of the head of him that was separate from his brethren " (Gen. xlix. 22-26).

" And of Joseph he said, Blessed of the Lord be his land, for the precious things of heaven, for the dew, and for the deep that coucheth beneath, And for the precious fruits brought forth by the sun, and for the precious things put forth by the moon, And for the chief things of the ancient mountains, and for the precious things of the lasting hills, And for the precious things of the earth and fulness thereof, and for the good will of him that dwelt in the bush: let the blessing come upon the head of Joseph, and upon the top of the head of him that was separated from his brethren. His glory is like the firstling of his bullock, and his horns are like the horns of unicorns: with them he shall push the people together to the ends of the earth: and they are the ten thousands of Ephraim, and they are the thousands of Manasseh " (Deut. xxxiii. 13-17).

What history! What experience!! What blessings!!! The life of Joseph is so abundant that one could readily write a book, but one must not be side-tracked from the present study on the Priestly Garments, nor forget that this character is only a parenthesis.

HIS BIRTH. "*And God remembered Rachel.*" Joseph, like Samuel, was an answer to prayer, but Rachel thought that God had forgotten her. Delayed answers to prayer may be for testings of faith. They are evidence of God's intense interest, not of His indifference. Joseph came, the man who was doubly fruitful. He came at the right time to save his people from the results of famine. Joseph was born for a purpose, Jesus was born for a purpose, you and I are born for a purpose. Life is no chance.

His name meaning " Doubly Fruitful ", we find that Joseph has a double representation on the Breastplate in the names of his two sons, Ephraim and Manasseh.

THE PATRIARCHAL BLESSING " *Joseph is a fruitful bough.*" An examination of his life will reveal that he was a character that produced the whole of the Fruit of the Spirit — Love in his whole life, Joy in family renewal, Peace of heart whilst in prison, Long-suffering towards a forgetful butler, Gentleness when his brethren were cruel, Goodness in his home life, Faith in his God at all times, Meekness in his dreams, and Temperance in Potiphar's house. These qualities could be seen everywhere.

" *Even a fruitful bough by a well.*" The secret of his fruitfulness was his position, " *planted by the rivers of water*", his spiritual roots in the place of abundant supply. Rooted and grounded in love. " *Whose branches run over the wall.*" The picture of usefulness. It is one thing to live a Christian life inside the Church and among fellow Christians, it is another thing to bear fruit in the home, the business, the world. Our branches must go over the wall so that fainting souls ⸺ y pick of the fruit of our experience.

" *The archers have sorely grieved him, and shot at him, and hated him.*" Did not the Lord say, " In the world ye shall have tribulation?" Well-placed roots are an essential but not the only one. Pruning, too, is necessary — no pruning, no fruit; no warfare, no victory; no trial, no faith. Joseph was " grieved " by misunderstanding, " shot at " by hurling accusations, " hated " by brethren, mistress and master, but he was *" made strong by the hands of the mighty God of Jacob "*. " No weapon that is formed against thee shall prosper " is the promise of Scripture. Joseph proved it, we may prove it. So he advanced until he was second ruler in the land and was enjoying all the blessings that are enumerated in the text. Made strong and finding favour because blessed by the Loving God of Abraham, the Faithful God of Isaac, the Mighty God of Jacob, and the Protecting God of Joseph.

THE MOSAIC BLESSING. The blessing bestowed by Moses upon Joseph as a people is in harmony and accord with that bestowed upon Joseph as an individual by Jacob. At first casual reading it might almost appear to be a repetition, and yet there is a great fundamental difference between the two. In Genesis all the blessings of heaven and earth, blessings past, present, and future, are bestowed upon Joseph, but here in Deuteronomy similar abundance is bestowed upon his land — notice *v.* 13. " And of Joseph he said, Blessed of the Lord be HIS LAND . . . " The man rooted and grounded in God is the man who finds that he is not only enriched in spiritual things but also in the realm of the material. Is this not the suggestion of the Psalmist in his first Psalm? " And he shall be like a tree planted by the rivers of water, that bringeth forth his fruit (spiritual) in his season; his leaf (material) also shall not wither; and *whatsoever* (spiritual and material) he doeth shall prosper."

CHAPTER XXII

URIM AND THUMMIM

Exod. xxviii. 30; *Lev.* viii. 8; *Num.* xxvii. 21; *Deut.* xxxiii. 8; 1 *Sam.* xxviii. 6; xxx. 7-8; *Ezra* ii. 63; *Neh.* vii. 65.

" And thou shalt put in the Breastplate of judgment the Urim and the Thummim; and they shall be upon Aaron's heart, when he goeth in before the Lord : and Aaron shall hear the judgment of the children of Israel upon his heart before the Lord continually " (Exod. xxviii. 30).

WE NOW turn to that which appears to many to be the mystery of all mysteries! How often is the question asked as to what are the Urim and the Thummim. There are numerous answers given both as to their appearance and as to their method of operation. None of these do we purpose to recount here (they may be read in various Commentaries if desired). The majority of ideas is mere speculation without any given reason. It is our desire to propound a further theory but, at the same time, add to it a weight of reason that will at least give it some authority; nevertheless one feels that none of us can speak with a certainty. It appears to be one of the things that God has hidden from us for the time being to be some of that " hidden manna " upon which we shall feast in the eternity when " we shall know even as we are known ".

Before outlining the suggestion of this we are assured that the two words mean — " Urim, Lights; Thummim, Perfection." We know, too, that Christ is light, for in Him there is no darkness at all. He is the light of life, the light of understanding, and the light of revelation.

Also Christ is perfect. All things were made by Him and for Him, and without Him was not anything made that was made. He is the Alpha and Omega, the beginning and the end of all things. To none other could be committed the work of " judgment ".

One of the first principles of Bible interpretation is to understand that it is an Eastern Book, lived and written in the environment of Palestine life and habit, and also that every illustration used by God in the Old Testament, was an illustration readily discerned by man because of common use. If this were not so then it is not an illustration, for such are always given for clarity not for complication.

The suggestion is made therefore that Urim and Thummim were in the form of a black and white stone deposited within the Breastplate; the black stone being the negative and the white stone being the positive, because the use of the black and white stones was common to those people in those days and therefore they would fully understand their implications.

This can be worked out to an issue both in Eastern custom and in Biblical record. It is to be realised that the casting of lots holds a prominence in the Scriptures. This, of course, does not fall into the same category as the gambling of modern days, and in no wise justifies the luck believed in by a superstitious generation such as ours. There were evil men, like the hard and callous soldiers, who cast lots for the garment of the Lord, there were superstitious sailors who cast lots to find out the cause of the storm in the experiences of Jonah. On the other hand there were the honest and noble disciples who cast lots for the choosing of Matthias for apostleship, as well as the High Priests who, seemingly, sought the mind of the Lord in a similar fashion. Most of the vices of to-

day are an abuse of something once given for man's use!
The action of the apostles was one of prayer, and then
belief in Divine Guidance. So much for the casting of
lots, now for something of the method employed. In
Rev. ii. 17 we read : " He that hath an ear, let him hear
what the Spirit saith unto the Churches; To him that
overcometh will I give to eat of the hidden manna, and
will give him a white stone, and in the stone a new
name written, which no man knoweth saving he that
receiveth it." Here is a Scriptural clue to the black and
white stone, for what was this white stone inscribed with
a name that was offered to the overcomer?

Black and white stones were used in many ways in the
East for the giving of a verdict. Here in this country,
in the Criminal Court, if a man is found guilty of mur-
der the Judge will don the black cap in pronouncing the
sentence of death. In a similar way in the East the Judge
would hand to the guilty prisoner a black stone, meaning
condemnation. Should the prisoner be handed a white
stone it would mean acquittal. In the election of magis-
trates and Officers of State, a number of black stones
would be put into a bag with one white stone on which
the name of the particular office was written. The number of stones would equal the number of nominees. These
would draw from the bag and the man obtaining the
white stone would gain the office. In a similar way men
would be admitted into certain secret societies.

Men would draw stones from a bag for the allocation
of portions of land for farming so that there would be
no unfairness in distribution. The white stone was given
to the winner of the ancient sports and races. It brought
him his reward. If one paused to comment on this in
relationship to the white stone of the overcomer in the
text of Revelation, it would be to say that those who

overcome " by the Blood of the Lamb and the word of their testimony " will receive the white stone of acquittal — justified; office — elected kings and priests; society — brought in His fellowship; land — an inheritance with the saints; reward — a crown of life.

It will readily be seen from the foregoing that these stones brought decision in matters of importance and that their usage was common. This being so there is some reason to suggest that Urim and Thummim, which were used as deciding factors to know the Will of God, might have been in this form. If this were so then the two stones, both of one size and shape, would lie deposited within the doubling of the Breastplate. When the Mind of God was wanted prayer would be offered, guidance sought, and then under that guidance the hand would be put in and a stone withdrawn. It might be well to point out that no conversation is recorded, but usually a positive or negative answer. The clearest Scripture on this point is 1 Sam. xxx. 7-8: " And David said to Abiathar, the priest, Ahimelech's son, I pray thee, bring me hither the ephod (The reason he asked for the ephod when he actually required Urim and Thummim was that Urim and Thummim were inside the Breastplate and the Breastplate was joined to the ephod at the shoulders by the shoulder stones. Therefore the whole must be brought so as to keep the Urim and Thummim secreted inside). And Abiathar brought thither the ephod to David. And David enquired at the Lord, saying, Shall I pursue after this troop? Shall I overtake them? And He answered him, Pursue: for thou shalt surely overtake them, and without fail recover all." In effect just the positive of the enquiry.

Even to-day when no Urim and Thummim are required, guidance is sought from the Holy Spirit, the

Third Person of the Holy Trinity, Who leads into all truth; and whilst we are sure of His Power and of His guidance, yet He remains indefinable. Therefore, whatever we may reason and however we may speculate, we must ultimately come back to the place in which we trust where we cannot trace.

The following from the pen of Dr. Joseph Parker is of practical and devotional value :

" What the Urim and the Thummim actually were no man has been able to find out. Whether they were to be used for the purpose of ascertaining the Divine will in critical and perplexing circumstances has been a question which has excited devout attention; but whatever the Urim and the Thummim were, there can be no doubt as to what our Urim and Thummim are. We are not left without light and perfection; we are not destitute of means of discovering the Divine purpose in our life and progress. Our Urim and Thummim are the Old and New Testaments. Keep these in the heart; be at home with them in all their wondrous variety of speech, of doctrine, of song, of inspiration, and of instruction of every kind; and then you never can stray far from the path providential that makes its own course straight up to the God Who started the mysterious outgoing. We have nothing to do with incantation; we do not go to consult the witch of Endor, the sorcerer, or the conjurer; we ask no questions at forbidden places. The whole life-course is mapped out in the Old Testament and in the New. The Testaments are never to be separated; they are to be read together, they explain one another; torn asunder, they lose their unity and their music; brought together, you bring flower to the root, you bring the noonday to the dawn, you unite things, forces, ministries that ought never to be dissevered. Let the word of Christ dwell in you richly. Scripture given by inspiration is profitable for all the necessities of life. If we stray, it is not for want of light; if we persist in obeying our own perverted instincts and impulses, we must not be surprised that we end in the bog of despair or in the wilderness of destitution. Do not move without consulting the oracle Divine. Let our motto be, ' To the law, and to the testimony ', and what cannot be confirmed by the spirit of the book is unworthy to be admitted into our life as an inspiring and directing force."

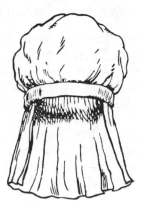

THE MITRE.

CHAPTER XXIII

THE MITRE AND BONNET

Exod. xxviii. 39-40; xxxix. 28

" . . . and thou shalt make the mitre of fine linen, and thou shalt make the girdle of needlework. And for Aaron's sons thou shalt make coats, and thou shalt make for them girdles, and bonnets shalt thou make for them, for glory and for beauty " (Exod. xxviii. 39-40).
" And a mitre of fine linen, and goodly bonnets of fine linen . . . " (Exod. xxxix. 28).

VERY LITTLE is said concerning the mitre and no description is given of its shape, yet there is enough to bring before our notice some important principles.

Let it be observed that there was a distinction between the headdress of the High Priest and that of the priests. In the case of the High Priest it was a mitre, whilst his sons wore bonnets. The bonnet was seemingly in the form of a turban for the word " put " in Exod. xxix. 9, where we read : " And put the bonnets on them," is the word " bind " in the original.

In both cases the headdress was made of fine linen as was the coat, so that the head was crowned with the symbol of holiness and righteousness.   An important factor for those who hold the responsibility of leadership, and particularly those who lead in religious affairs.   This was decidedly true of the Lord Jesus Christ, our Great High Priest.   His was holiness in the deepest and fullest sense of the word.

The head is that which denotes authority. It is the head that controls the whole of the body. Christ as the Head of the Church controls that Church. But again, the head becomes the emblem of wisdom. H. W. Soltau points out how well this is illustrated in the Scriptures. It is in par-ticular the hoary head that speaks of wisdom because wisdom is obtained by experience and so we read in the Proverbs : " The hoary (white) head is a crown of glory, if it be found in the way of righteousness " (Prov. xvi. 31), and " . . . the beauty of old men is the grey head " (Prov. xx. 29).   Old age and white hair tell of a life lived, experience gained, and wisdom obtained, which means that such should have the power to impart wis-dom.   Our minds are led back to the story in the Old Testament concerning Rehoboam, the king of Israel, who consulted with the old men as to how he should govern his people.   They advised him on the ground of their experience, but he forsook their wisdom and sought the guidance of the young men who had little knowledge of the true facts and their advice proved to be folly (see 1 Kings xii).

Whilst generally speaking, wisdom is found with maturity, our Lord never reached those years which are rich with experience. He never gained the beauty that belongs to age, for He was cut off in the midst of His days — a young Man in the prime of life. It is becoming, therefore, to find the Lord referred to as the " Ancient of days " in Dan. vii. 9. " I beheld till the thrones were cast down, and the Ancient of days did sit, whose garment was white as snow, and the hair of his head like the pure wool . . . " Again the Lord is seen in the midst of the seven candlesticks which were for the seven Churches. He is there in administrative power. " His head and His hairs were white like wool, as white as snow . . . " (Rev. i. 14). It is from the white head being the symbol of wisdom and understanding that has developed the white wig now worn by Judges and others in the Courts of our land. This white headdress of wisdom belonged to High Priest and Priest alike. Two references will suffice to reveal this truth — firstly, concerning Him Who is our Great High Priest, " He is made unto us wisdom (the mitre), righteousness (the coat), sanctification (the golden plate), and redemption (the Breastplate); secondly, concerning ourselves as priests, James says : " If any of you lack wisdom, let him ask God, that giveth to all men liberally, and upbraideth not; and it shall be given him " (James i. 5).

The word " bonnet " is derived from a word which means " to elevate " or " lift up ". How suggestive ! Only the priests wore this, not the High Priest. Has not Christ our Great High Priest lifted us to heavenly places and made us kings and priests unto Him? Not one of us was of ourselves worthy of such honour. He humbled Himself that we might be exalted. Let us therefore walk worthy of the vocation to which we have been called.

Whilst the bonnet may be derived from that which

means elevation, yet the real reason for wearing bonnet or mitre was to cover the head because of being in the presence of an Holy God, the covering of the head always signifying subjection. The Lord Jesus was ever subjected to His Father and His Father's Will. " For I came down from heaven not to do mine own will, but the will of Him that sent Me " (John vi. 38). " Wist ye not that I must be about My Father's business?" (Luke ii. 49). " Nevertheless not My will, but Thine, be done " (Luke xxii. 42).

It was ever customary for the Jew to cover his head and uncover his feet when entering the synagogue, or when praying, or reading the law or the prophets, their sacred books. This was a recognition of the majesty of God, His greatness and their unworthiness; not a cowed attitude of fear crouching under a hard master, but the willing subjection of reverence and holy love. This is the subjection referred to in Eph. v. 22-24 : " Wives, submit yourselves unto your own husbands, as unto the Lord. For the husband is the head of the wife, even as Christ is the Head of the Church : and He is the Saviour of the body. Therefore as the Church is subject unto Christ, so let the wives be to their own husbands in everything. Husbands love your wives."

In the New Testament the method is changed. The man now uncovers his head and keeps his feet covered, instead of covering his head and uncovering his feet as God said to Moses : " . . . put off thy shoes from off thy feet, for the place whereon thou standest is holy ground " (Exod. iii. 5). Because the woman covered her head, regulations were laid down to the Corinthian Church : " Every man praying or prophesying, having his head covered, dishonoureth his head. But every woman that prayeth or prophesieth with her head uncovered dishonoureth her head . . . judge in yourselves : is it comely that a woman pray unto God uncovered?" (1 Cor. ii. 4-13).

These Scriptures are written for our learning. Therefore it ought to be understood that herein lies a principle. Unworthy men must approach an holy God in an attitude which recognises His dignity and authority. Changing scenes and times may alter the mode of acknowledgment, as can readily be seen between Old and New Testament times, but this neither justifies nor excuses the non-wearing of hats by women in our Church Services to-day; because to-day's attitude is not the changing of the method of acknowledgment of God but the entire abandonment of any act of recognition which means an undermining of principle itself; and when we forsake principles we forsake foundations, and when foundations are removed whole structures fall. Let us therefore not be wise in our own conceits, but let us enjoy the adornment of that wisdom of which James says "But the wisdom that is from above is first pure, then peaceable, gentle, and easy to be intreated, full of mercy and good fruits, without partiality, and without hypocrisy" (James iii. 17).

THE HOLY CROWN

CHAPTER XXIV

THE HOLY CROWN

Exod. xxviii. 36-38; xxxix. 30-31

" And thou shalt make a plate of pure gold, and grave upon it, like the engravings of a signet, HOLINESS TO THE LORD. And thou shalt put it on a blue lace, that it may be upon the mitre; upon the forefront of the mitre it shall be. And it shall be upon Aaron's forehead, that Aaron may bear the iniquity of the holy things, which the children of Israel shall hallow in all their holy gifts; and it shall be always upon his forehead, that they may be accepted before the Lord " (Exod. xxviii. 36-38).

" And they made the plate of the holy crown of pure gold, and wrote upon it a writing, like to the engravings of a signet, HOLINESS TO THE LORD. And they tied unto it a lace of blue, to fasten it on high upon the mitre; as the Lord commanded Moses " (Exod. xxxix. 30-31).

THE HEBREW word here translated " plate " is " tsits " and elsewhere is translated " flower " and " blossom ", as in the flowers (tsits) which adorned the pillars of Solomon's Temple — Jachin and Boaz. The flowers that wreathed those massive pillars of strength added beauty, a grace, a charm, as did the holy crown upon the brow of the High Priest, and as does the holiness that hallows

the head of the believer. It is also found in Ps. ciii. 15:
" As for man, his days are as grass: as the flower (tsits)
of the field, so he flourisheth." Isaiah says: " Whose
glorious beauty is a fading flower (tsits) (xxviii. 1), and
" All flesh is grass, and all the goodliness thereof is as
the flower (tsits) of the field. The grass withereth, the
flower (tsits) fadeth . . . " (xl. 6-8).

Here in Exodus xxviii. 36 it is " Thou shalt make a
plate (tsits) of pure gold." Might this not suggest the
thought that man at his best, when he has entered into
the full bloom of life, is enjoying the flower of manhood,
is full of his own self-importance, and is boasting of all
his glory and beauty, is no more than a fading flower?
He has nothing he can retain. To-day the grass is, and
to-morrow it is cast into the oven. To-day man is, to-
morrow he hastens into eternity. Perhaps it ought to be
explained that the grass of the field in Palestine, and therefore in the Bible, is not limited to the grass of field and
meadow in the sense that we understand grass, but it
refers to all that springs up out of the ground of its own
accord. It includes all wild flowers, and there are many
in that country, hence the references to the beauty and
to the wind passing over it and it is gone and the place
thereof shall know it no more. Against all this brevity,
uncertainty, and fading, there stands in contrast that
lasting beauty, that glorious certainty, that permanent
quality that belongeth to the man whose life is crowned
with the fragrant blossom of holiness. On the Great
High Priest we see the unfading flower of pure gold
which adorns the brow that once was pierced with thorns.

Notice further the position of this crown of glory that
rests upon the foundation of a spotless righteousness of
which the mitre is made — " And it shall be upon
Aaron's forehead." The forehead is the seat of the will

and of the intellect. The determination of that will and the character of that mind indelibly inscribe themselves upon the forehead, so that it can truthfully be said that an inscription is written upon every forehead. You have heard it said, possibly said it yourself about someone: " I can read him like a book," but always remember that if it is true then the other person can read you like a book. This should bring an important enquiry from us — if he can, then what does he read?

On seeing a person with a high forehead, like that of Caesar, the remark is passed that that man has a large brain, he is a thinker. Another has a wrinkled brow and those wrinkles spell out the word " worry ". When the forehead is dropped stern determination is detected. These are always plainly read inscriptions, often unconsciously inscribed. A few Scriptures to bear out the same thought. Jer. iii. 3: " . . . thou hadst a whore's forehead . . . " This was said to Israel and Judah concerning their idolatry and rebellion. Ezek. iii. 7: " . . . for all the house of Israel are stiff of forehead, and hard of heart (margin)". Then in the next verses: " I have made thy forehead strong against their foreheads . . . as an adamant harder than flint have I made thy forehead . . . " The Lord is here telling Ezekiel that stubbornness is the character of the nation. There was no bending of their wills, but God would make His prophet as determined in ministering the Word as they were in refusing it. Rev. xvii. 5: " And upon her forehead was a name written, MYSTERY, BABYLON THE GREAT, THE MOTHER OF HARLOTS AND ABOMINATIONS OF THE EARTH."

Lev. xiii. teaches that there were many forms of leprosy. Each had to be treated differently. One of these kinds was leprosy in the forehead (*vv.* 42-46), and this was the worst with which man could be defiled. Verse 44 says that the priest shall pronounce him *utterly* unclean. He was the only man that had to put his hand over his mouth and cry: "Unclean, unclean!" He was the man who had to live in absolute isolation right outside the camp. In this connection there is an extraordinary illustration in 2 Chron. xxvi where the story is told of good King Uzziah. He reigned fifty-two years in Jerusalem and did much that was highly commendable until, in the hour of his strength, pride took hold of him and in his pride he entered the Temple of the Lord to burn incense. This was a privilege that never fell to kings to perform. It was the peculiar ministry of the priests and that by Divine ordination. Azariah, the priest, went in with his colleagues to forbid the king his act of desecration and to warn him of the penalty, but pride was ruling. The king would not be deterred but rather showed his anger at being reproved and we read: ". . . and while he was wroth with the priests, the leprosy even rose in his forehead . . . and they thrust him out from thence; yea, himself hasted also to go out, because the Lord had smitten him. And Uzziah the king was a leper until the day of his death, and dwelt in a several house, being a leper; for he was cut off from the house of the Lord . . . " The pride, arrogancy, and self-will of his mind wrote themselves upon his forehead in the dread disease of leprosy.

What have we written on our forehead? The High Priest bore the inscription HOLINESS TO THE LORD. This is the crowning fact, the culmination of everything. Without this " all else is worthless — forms, ceremonies, priestly attire, sacrifice, prayer, are mockeries. It required primarily the high priest himself to be holy; but it was a call also to the whole nation, whose representative the high priest was, that they should be ' a holy nation ', ' a kingdom of priests ', and should consecrate themselves heart and soul to Jehovah " (Ellicott).

To have HOLINESS TO THE LORD written upon the flower of life, upon that which is best, upon our intellect, upon our character, is to have it written everywhere; for here it must affect the labours of our hands, here it must influence the utterances of our lips, here it must control the path of our feet, here it must sweeten the influence we radiate. But not any of these things is ours by merit. This inscription did not belong to the priests of the Old Testament, only to the High Priest, and yet to-day these things can be ours. They are to be ours because the Lord said : " Be ye holy even as I am holy."

This crown with its inscription was secured by a ribband of blue. Aaron could only bear the iniquity of the holy things as the honour, privilege, and responsibility, were conferred upon him by the grace of God. Jesus was holy by Divine right. Blue is the typological colour of both grace and Divinity.

> " Write upon our garnered treasures
>   Write on our choicest pleasures,
>   Upon things new and old;
>   The precious stone and gold —
>   Wife, husband, children, friends —
>   On all that goodness lends;
>   Go write on your good name —
>   Upon your cherished fame —
>   On every pleasant thing —
>   On stores that heaven doth fling
>   Into your basket — write !
>   Upon the smile of God,
>   Upon His scourging rod —

Write on your inmost heart,
Write upon every part —
To Him who claims the whole,
Time, talent, body, soul —
HOLINESS UNTO THE LORD!

CHAPTER XXV

THE BREECHES

Exodus xxviii. 42-43; *Lev.* vi. 8-10; xvi. 4; *Ezek.* xliv. 18

" And thou shalt make them linen breeches to cover their nakedness; (M. flesh of their nakedness) from the loins even unto the thighs they shall reach: And they shall be upon Aaron, and upon his sons, when they come in unto the tabernacle of the congregation, or when they come near unto the altar to minister in the holy place; that they bear not iniquity, and die: it shall be a statute for ever unto him and his seed after him " (Exod. xxviii. 42-43).

" And the Lord spake unto Moses, saying, Command Aaron and his sons, saying, This is the law of the burnt offering: It is the burnt offering, because of the burning upon the altar all night unto the morning, and the fire of the altar shall be burning in it. And the priest shall put on his linen garment, and his linen breeches shall be put upon his flesh, and take up the ashes which the fire hath consumed with the burnt offering on the altar, and he shall put them beside the altar " (Lev. xi. 8-10).

THE LAST verses of Exodus xxviii. are just a summary of what remains of the vestments of the ordinary priests, coats, girdles, and bonnets, all of the same material as the High Priest but just a little different in detail.

Then, finally, we are introduced to one more garment common to all and essential to all. They were to wear breeches or drawers made of linen. Whilst it was customary for the Egyptians to wear this garment, it was not so with the peoples of many nations and particularly so in the conducting of worship to their heathen gods. Much of the idol worship was sensual, sexual, obscene, and nakedness was often part of their conduct. For the worshipper of God there must be modesty and decency, for we must worship Him in the beauty of holiness.

We observe that this particular garment was to be worn when coming into the Tabernacle of the congregation or when approaching the altar to minister in the holy place. Worship and service must be according to the prescribed method given by God or else death will be the result. Matthew Henry, who always had an unique way of expressing things, puts it thus: " Those who are guilty of omission in duty as well as omission of duty, shall bear their iniquity. If the priests perform the instituted service, and do not do it in the appointed garments, it is (say the Jewish doctors) as if a stranger did it, and the stranger that comes nigh shall be put to death. Nor will God connive at the presumptions and irreverences even of those whom He causes to draw most near to Him: if Aaron himself put a slight upon the divine institution, he shall bear iniquity and die." Is this the reason why so much of our christian worship is formal and lifeless? Is this the cause of so much, of our christian service being fruitless and dead? We must not only do the thing that God requires of us but we must also do it in the way He desires. Let us examine our conduct, our methods, in the light of this revelation, for whilst this in particular is an Old Testament requirement under the law, it can be seen in principle to be a New Testament requirement under Grace.

The subject of holiness, which finds its culmination in the Holy Plate which is secured to the brow of the High Priest, has a development of thought as it is seen typified in each of the garments made of the fine twined linen, giving us an appreciation of the term " Holy Garments ". The coat that clad his person would signify an holiness of the heart that beat beneath it. The girdle that bound up his loins would suggest an holiness of the service rendered to the Lord. The mitre that adorned his head would speak of holiness of thought and control, whilst these linen breeches that covered his nakedness declare an holiness of the flesh. Yes, the breeches mean just that — the covering of the flesh. Through the flesh, its desires and passions, sin operates. The Apostle reminds us in Galatians v. what the works of the flesh are — " Adultery, fornication, uncleanness, lasciviousness, idolatry, witchcraft, hatred, variance, emulations, wrath, strife, seditions, heresies, envyings, murders, drunkenness, revellings, and suchlike. . . . " No wonder he said in Romans vii. 18: " For I know that in me (that is, in my flesh) dwelleth no good thing . . . " It was through the flesh, the lust of the flesh, the lust of the eyes, and the pride of life, that Eve and Adam fell and, having done so, they sought to cover the flesh with their home-made aprons but without success. God sees all, God knows all, and God made the adequate provision. With the sanctified life engaged in the service of the Lord there must be no provision made for the flesh. The Lord has made the covering, and to approach the holy place or altar without it is death.

We will end our studies of the Priestly Garments with the Word of the Lord:

" There is therefore no condemnation to them which are in Christ Jesus, who walk not after the flesh, but after the Spirit. For the law of the Spirit of life in Christ Jesus hath made me free from the law of sin and death. For what the law could not do, in that it was weak through the flesh, God sending His own Son in the likeness of sinful flesh and for sin, condemned sin in the flesh: That the righteousness of the law might be fulfilled in us, who walk not after the flesh, but after the Spirit. For they that are after the flesh do mind the things of the flesh, but they that are after the Spirit the things of the Spirit. For to be carnally minded is death; but to be spiritually minded is life and peace. Because the carnal mind is enmity against God: for it is not subject to the law of God, neither indeed can be. So then they that are in the flesh cannot please God. But ye are not in the flesh, but in the Spirit, if so be that the Spirit of God dwell in you. Now if any man hath not the Spirit of Christ, he is none of His. And if Christ be in you, the body is dead because of sin; but the Spirit is life because of righteousness. But if the Spirit of Him that raised up Jesus from the dead dwell in you, He that raised up Christ from the dead shall also quicken your mortal bodies by His Spirit that dwelleth in you. Therefore, brethren, we are debtors, not to the flesh, to live after the flesh. For if ye live after the flesh, ye shall die: but if ye through the Spirit do mortify the deeds of the body, ye shall live. For as many as are led by the Spirit of God, they are the sons of God." (Romans viii. 1-14.)